Magdalen College Occa

Series Editor C. Y. F

with best wishes

[illegible]

16th June 1999

Education in Early Tudor England

Magdalen College Oxford and Its School 1480–1540

NICHOLAS ORME

Magdalen College · Oxford
1998

ISBN 0 9513747 4 5

CONTENTS

ILLUSTRATIONS

ACKNOWLEDGEMENTS

The author and publisher are grateful to the University of Exeter and to the Richard III and Yorkist History Trust for grants towards the preparation and publication of the plates and text figures in this book. They are also indebted to the following for permission to reproduce illustrations: the Dean and Chapter of Winchester Cathedral (Fig. 1); the Bibliothèque d'Arras, France (Fig. 3); the British Library (Fig. 16); and the Bibliographical Society (Figs 17, 18, 19).

PREFACE

The early Tudor period, from about 1480 to 1540, was an important time of change in English school education. This was the era when Latin ceased to be taught as it had been in the later middle ages and came to be modelled on 'humanist' Latin, meaning the Latin of classical Rome. A leading role in this change was played by Magdalen College Oxford and by its grammar school, now Magdalen College School, founded in 1480. The school's first masters — John Anwykyll, John Holt, and John Stanbridge — were among the earliest men in England to teach humanist Latin in the classroom and to write textbooks about it. Their work helped bring about the cultural changes in England that are associated with the Renaissance. Thomas Wolsey, another early master of the school, had a different but equally important influence on education. He founded a major English school at Ipswich and, as a leader of the English Church, made the first attempts to establish a national curriculum for grammar schools in England.

The importance of Magdalen College School as a pioneer centre of humanism has long been recognized. As early as the 1670s, Anthony Wood pointed out the influence of its masters on Latin teaching in England and began to reconstruct their careers.[1] In the nineteenth century, J.R. Bloxam and W.D. Macray did archival research on the early history of the college and its members,[2] and A.B. Emden built on their work in his biographical registers of Oxford men published in 1957–74.[3] A good history of the school was written by R.S. Stanier in 1940 and revised in 1958.[4] Modern historians of education have generally endorsed the school's leading role in the Renaissance period,[5] so it is fair to ask if there is

[1] Anthony Wood, *The History and Antiquities of the Colleges and Halls in the University of Oxford*, ed. by J. Gutch, 5 vols (Oxford, 1786–90), I, 351, 627; *Athenae Oxonienses*, ed. by P. Bliss, 4 vols (London, 1813–20), I, cols 14–15 (John Holt).

[2] J.R. Bloxam, *A Register of the Presidents, Fellows, Demies . . . and Other Members of St Mary Magdalen College in the University of Oxford*, 8 vols (Oxford, 1853–85); W.D. Macray, *A Register of the Members of St. Mary Magdalen College, Oxford*, n.s., 8 vols (London, 1894–1915).

[3] A.B. Emden, *A Biographical Register of the University of Oxford to A.D. 1500*, 3 vols (Oxford, 1957–59) (hereafter *BRUO* I–III); *A Biographical Register of the University of Oxford A.D. 1501 to 1540* (Oxford, 1974) (hereafter *BRUO* IV).

[4] R.S. Stanier, *A History of Magdalen College School, Oxford*, 2nd edn (Oxford, 1958).

[5] E.g. A.F. Leach, *The Schools of Medieval England*, 2nd edn (London, 1915), pp. 271–72; K. Charlton, *Education in Renaissance England* (London, 1965), p. 106; John Lawson and Harold Silver, *A Social History of Education in England* (London, 1973), p. 51; Nicholas Orme, *English Schools in the Middle Ages* (London, 1973), esp. pp. 107–11.

anything new to be said. In fact there is a great deal. At the most basic level of fact, the lists of schoolmasters and ushers printed by Bloxam and Stanier contain errors of names and dates which need correction. Much more can be said about their owners' identities and careers, thanks to Emden's biographical researches. The archives of Magdalen College contain more information than has hitherto been exploited, notably plans and pictures of the school building — rare evidence about the architecture of a late medieval school. Another school-text has been found which reflects the work of the Magdalen classroom, and more research has been done on the history of school education in England since Stanier's time. We are now better able to measure Magdalen's achievements against that history.

The present study seeks to make available this new information in a fuller and more accurate history of the school's first 60 years. It also aims to improve our knowledge of Tudor school education. The resources for studying Magdalen School are exceptionally good. Apart from a few other places like Eton, St Paul's, and Winchester College, no other early Tudor school has left so much evidence of its activities. Scarcely anywhere else can such a full account be given of a school's foundation, organization, masters, pupils, buildings, and curriculum. It follows that studying Magdalen School reveals a great many features of education in early Tudor England, and illuminates them from the school's own records. Rarely can schools of the period, except for those mentioned above, be shown to have exerted so much influence outside their immediate localities. Not only were Anwykyll, Holt, Stanbridge, and Wolsey figures of national importance, but many lesser-known masters and pupils of Magdalen School, by moving elsewhere, helped to spread humanist learning across England. Further still, the activities of the school's alumni contributed to the development of printing, uniformity, and royal education in the first half of the sixteenth century.

I have been studying Magdalen School and its early Tudor counterparts for many years, in tandem with other research, and my first obligation is to thank the President and Fellows of Magdalen for their generosity in providing accommodation in the college, access to its archives, and space for this book in its series of publications. My thanks are also due to Magdalen College School, Mr Peter Tinniswood, and Mr Andrew Halls for their interest in and affirmation of the project. I am especially grateful to Mrs J.A. Dettmar of Magdalen for arranging my stays there, to the college archivists Dr Janie Cottis and Dr Robin Darwall-Smith for much courteous help, and to Dr Christine Ferdinand, Fellow Librarian of the college, for her pains as general editor of the book and for her constant encouragement. I am indebted to Mr Peter Northeast for useful information about Andrew Scarbot, to Dr Gerald Harriss for reading a draft of the book and contributing helpful advice, and to Mr M. Rouillard for drawing the three text-figures to his usual high standard. Finally, any abilities that I have as an historian owe much to the late K.B. McFarlane, my tutor at Magdalen, and to the late Dr A.B. Emden, a generous friend and supporter of younger scholars including myself. Throughout my work on this study they have often returned to my mind, and I offer it to their memory with gratitude.

NICHOLAS ORME

FIG. 1. The tomb of William Waynflete (d. 1486) in Winchester Cathedral. An angel displays the coat of arms of the bishop and of his college.

1. MAGDALEN COLLEGE SCHOOL: ITS FOUNDATION AND CONTEXT

William Waynflete and His Foundations

William Waynflete (*c.*1400–86), headmaster of Winchester College, provost of Eton, bishop of Winchester, and chancellor of England, was the kind of man whose curriculum vitae appears to demonstrate an effortless rise to greatness through exceptional talents.[6] In fact, he owed his eminence to a remarkable piece of luck rather than to his own abilities. William was born at Wainfleet (Lincolnshire) into a family of respectable but modest importance. The social status of his father, William Patten, who also called himself Barbour, is unclear; his mother Margaret is said to have been a gentleman's daughter. The family's rank seems to have been at best that of lesser gentry, perhaps even lower, and William did not adopt either of his father's surnames. Little is known about his education. He is unlikely to have studied at Winchester College, as used to be thought; a Lincolnshire grammar school is more probable. He appears to have gone on to study at Oxford, where he may have taken an MA degree, but he does not emerge clearly in records until his appointment as headmaster of Winchester College in June 1430.

This post tells us something about his abilities; it also confirms the impression of his moderate social origins. Schoolmasters in the early fifteenth century were not important men. Most of them worked for fees, but Winchester was unusual in paying its master a stipend of £10 to teach its pupils free of charge. The hours were long, the work hard, and the esteem low. Laymen who took up teaching usually did so as a long-term career; it had the advantage over the priesthood of allowing one to marry. Clerics who taught (and Waynflete took holy orders) usually hoped to acquire a patron who would appoint them to a parish living. When that happened, they turned with gratitude to the quieter, more respected life of a rector or vicar. It followed that gentlemen's sons did not become schoolmasters, because the work offered insufficient wealth, position, or advancement. Rather, the occupation attracted sons of yeomen or burgesses with lower expectations. True, Winchester College was an important foundation, but it had only two teachers (a headmaster and an usher) and it did not yet

[6] The best survey of Waynflete's life is now Virginia Davis, *William Waynflete: Bishop and Educationalist* (Woodbridge, 1993).

possess its later prestige as a great national public school. In 1430 it was still obliged to appoint an outsider like Waynflete to be headmaster; not until about 1450 did it have enough good candidates from its own alumni to stop taking anyone else. Waynflete stayed in office for 11 years: another point of significance. Either he was a career schoolmaster, willing to spend his life in the classroom, or he was unsuccessful in gaining patronage. He did, in fact, receive an appointment from Cardinal Beaufort, the bishop of Winchester, as master of the small hospital of St Mary Magdalene outside the city, which he held together with the school. But though he evidently had good standing locally, he did not possess enough to be given a major promotion.

The accident that caused Waynflete's career to take off was due to the king, Henry VI. Born in December 1421 and made king nine months later, he reached the age of seventeen in 1439 and began to rule for himself. Henry has come down in history with a reputation for holiness and he was indeed a devout man, but so were many kings. What made him unique was his interest in schools.[7] No previous ruler, as far as we know, had been concerned with such places in more than a casual way, whereas one of Henry's first actions on taking control of affairs in 1439 was to plan an ambitious new school at Eton near his castle of Windsor. The fact that William Bingham, a London cleric, asked for his help in the same year to establish a college at Cambridge to train schoolmasters, shows that the king's educational leanings were widely known.[8] Once the foundation of Eton had begun, Henry decided to visit Winchester College to see a similar kind of institution. He went there in August 1441 and, although we do not know what happened between him and Waynflete, the two must have formed an instant and close relationship. Within about a month, Waynflete gave up his headmastership and was promoted by Henry as provost of Eton College in charge of setting up the new foundation. Five and a half years later, Cardinal Beaufort died on 11 April 1447. That very same day, when the king heard the news, he wrote to the monks of Winchester Cathedral asking them to elect Waynflete as bishop of Winchester. The ex-schoolmaster was raised to one of the most senior and wealthy posts in the Church of England, solely through the king's favour, without having played any major role in national affairs.

Biographically, then, it is not surprising that a man who owed his eminence to schoolteaching should have founded an Oxford college that also included a

[7] See Orme, *English Schools*, pp. 197–99, and idem, *Education and Society in Medieval and Renaissance England* (London, 1989), p. 14.

[8] On Bingham, see A.H. Lloyd, *The Early History of Christ's College Cambridge* (Cambridge, 1934), passim.

school. For most of the college's history the school occupied a prominent place on its west side facing the High Street; it was moved to the other end of Magdalen Bridge only in 1928. Constitutionally, however, the incorporation of a grammar school with a university college was an unusual idea, hardly less remarkable in the fifteenth century than it would be today. One or two early Oxford colleges like Merton and Queen's had made arrangements for supporting a few boys, but the activities were on a small scale and the boys were likely to be sent out for teaching to a schoolmaster in Oxford. More recently, New College had included a group of choristers who needed education.[9] Magdalen College School, in contrast, was a much larger enterprise, meant not only for college members but for boys from outside the college. This was a novel arrangement. Even in the fifteenth century, educationists understood the difference between schools and universities, and normally kept them separate. Winchester College and New College Oxford were linked, and so were Eton College and King's College Cambridge, but they were miles apart from one another. Waynflete's foundation of a university college and a large school on the same site had no obvious model and inspired few imitations. One was Jesus College Cambridge which included a public grammar school in about 1500, and another was Trinity College Cambridge, founded in 1546.[10] But both their schools disappeared in the mid-sixteenth century, due to feelings that universities and schools were incongruous in close proximity. Similar criticisms were made of the Magdalen arrangement, as we shall see, and it survived only with some difficulty.[11]

Even Waynflete does not seem to have thought of combining a college and school in the first instance. He established the college in 1458 on the usual plan of a body of university scholars. Like New College, the foundation was a large one and, when fully developed, supported forty fellows and thirty undergraduate scholars or 'demies'.[12] William's interest in schools developed somewhat later and first took shape not in Oxford but at his birthplace, Wainfleet in Lincolnshire. In 1466–67 the college records refer to a man named John Marshall being paid £10 a year for teaching at Wainfleet in what became a

[9] Orme, *English Schools*, pp. 185–86.

[10] Ibid., pp. 210, 267.

[11] Below, p. 6.

[12] On the foundation of the college and its significance, see A.B. Cobban, *The Medieval English Universities: Oxford and Cambridge to c.1500* (Aldershot, 1988), passim, and J.I. Catto and Ralph Evans (eds), *The History of the University of Oxford*, II: *Late Medieval Oxford* (Oxford, 1992), 610–24.

permanent free grammar school.[13] The school in Oxford is not mentioned until 10 April 1478, when the university agreed to the following statute:

> that if any venerable man wishes to found a grammar school in which grammar shall be taught free to all wishing to come, then those teaching grammar in that school shall not be required to pay any sum to the university, and that the customary sum paid from ancient times shall be recovered from the other teachers of grammar.[14]

It had been customary for the university to levy a tax on schoolmasters in Oxford, because they taught for money. The statute of 1478 shows that, for the first time, a free grammar school was envisaged in the city. This school must have been Magdalen College School, and Waynflete must have approached the university to waive its tax, because we hear that the school was founded very soon after the 1478 statute. The early records of Magdalen College state that the college school opened at Easter 1480, when

> all and each were freely instructed in grammar at the expense of the lord founder by one master and an assistant, and this for a half year before [August 1480], namely from the previous Easter, in a certain lower hall in the college in an ancient building south of the chapel.[15]

There is no reason to believe, from this evidence, that the school is any older than 1480. It was apparently first held in a room in the college near the present High Street range of buildings, and then transferred to the west side of the college where it remained for the next 400 years.

In 1480, Waynflete issued a code of statutes for Magdalen College, one of which covered the school. It laid down that there should be a master and an usher (that is, an assistant master), appointed and removable by the president of the college. They were to give instruction freely and gratis, without any exaction (meaning fees), to anyone who came to the school. The master was to receive £10 a year and the usher £5, together with chambers and commons (daily food) equal to those given to the fellows of the college. The two teachers were required to give six months' notice of leaving, and the college had to give them three months' notice. Another teacher was to be provided within three days of a vacancy — a provision which seems to have been observed up to at least the 1540s, though it often involved the appointment of temporary staff until permanent ones could be found. The statute ended by forbidding any

[13] Brenda Parry-Jones and Derrick Wales, *Five Hundred Years of Magdalen College School Wainfleet 1484–1984* (Wainfleet, 1984), pp. 5, 7; Oxford, Magdalen College Archives (hereafter MCA), EP/165/6.

[14] *Statuta Antiqua Vniversitatis Oxon*, ed. by Strickland Gibson (Oxford, 1931), p. 291.

[15] MCA, Reg. A, fol. 3^r.

members of the college to impede the staff of the school in their work, or to obstruct the scholars from their learning without the president's permission.[16] College fellows were often tutors to scholars, who acted as part-time servants in return, and this part of the statute was probably meant to ensure that the scholars gave their day-time to studying rather than to menial jobs. The college accounts show that the commons were valued at a shilling a week, making the total earnings of the teachers £12 12*s*. and £7 12*s*. a year respectively: rates slightly better than the £10 and £5 a year normally paid to salaried masters and ushers in this period. There was no requirement that the school staff should be priests or laymen, graduates or non-graduates; they could and did belong to each of these categories.

The Purpose of the School

For whom did Waynflete provide his school? In the first place, it was to cater for the undergraduate members of the college — the thirty demies, or many of them. These youths were to spend their time learning grammar (involving how to understand, read, write, and speak Latin) and logic, and they were to be fully instructed in grammar before going on to logic.[17] The college also supported sixteen choristers (though it is not clear whether they had to study grammar), and certain other boys (perhaps as many as two or three dozen) boarded privately in the college with the fellows. Some of these boys too may have gone to the school.[18] The college, therefore, provided the core of the pupils but outsiders were eligible too, 'all those wishing to come' as the statutes put it. J.R. Bloxam, commenting on these words in 1863, declared firmly that 'the Founder did not, and could not, contemplate that any would resort to the Grammar School . . . except Academical persons belonging to the recognized class of Academical Grammar Scholars, and as such frequenting the School according to the discipline and usage of the University'.[19] In other words, he identified the outsiders with scholars from other university colleges. Bloxam, however, wrote when the university community was still relatively small and when it was very sensitive about its rights in relation to those of the city. It is likely, as he implies, that youths or men who were studying elsewhere in the university could gain

[16] G.R.M. Ward (ed.), *The Statutes of Magdalen College Oxford* (Oxford, 1840), pp. 58–59; *Statutes of the Colleges of Oxford* (Oxford and London, 1853), II, 76.
[17] *Statutes of the Colleges of Oxford* II, 6, 16.
[18] E.g. below, pp. 75–77.
[19] Bloxam, *Register*, III, 3–4.

admittance to the school. It is equally probable that some pupils came to the school from city families, as to a local grammar school.

There are two or three signs that citizens' sons came in. In some early Latin exercises associated with the school, a fictional pupil is imagined as having a cousin whose parents live in Oxford, so that the pupil himself (perhaps) was visualized as a local boy.[20] Dr Carl Hammer has drawn attention to the fact that Winchester College usually admitted one boy a year from Oxford in the 1460s and 1470s: boys likely to have been children of the tenants or servants of Winchester's sister foundation, New College Oxford. After 1477, however, these admissions virtually ceased for many years, which may indicate that such boys were being placed in Magdalen School instead.[21] The best evidence comes from the famous episode in 1550 when Dr Richard Coxe proposed, as part of the reform of the university by the government of Edward VI, that Magdalen College should no longer take pupils of grammar.[22] The college opposed this proposal successfully, and it was helped to do so by a letter from the mayor and corporation of Oxford to the Privy Council. The corporation argued that the university colleges had traditionally admitted children, 'some being called scholars of the Houses, and some called Choristers, and yet learning their grammar'. 'The most part' of these pupils, they claimed, were 'children of your said poor Orators [meaning the citizens], having of the said Colleges meat, drink, cloth, and lodging; and were very well brought up in learning in the common Grammar School at . . . Magdalen, and so went forward and attained to Logic, and other faculties'.[23] The words 'common grammar school' imply a school open to the public as well as to the university. Altogether, we should probably envisage Magdalen School receiving junior college members, members of other colleges, citizens' sons, and boys from elsewhere in England.[24] Town schools of this period, staffed by a master and usher like those of Magdalen,

[20] William Nelson (ed.), *A Fifteenth Century School Book* (Oxford, 1956), pp. 13–14 no. 52, pp. 15–18 nos. 55, pp. 60–66, 71.

[21] Carl J. Hammer, 'Oxford Town and Oxford University', in *The History of the University of Oxford*, III: *The Collegiate University*, ed. by James McConica (Oxford, 1986), 109–10; T.F. Kirby, *Winchester Scholars* (London and Winchester, 1888), esp. pp. 76–106.

[22] W.H. Frere and W.M. Kennedy (eds), *Visitation Articles and Injunctions of the Period of the Reformation* (1910), II, 229.

[23] Printed in Wood, *Colleges and Halls*, vol. II, col. 101, and Bloxam, *Register*, III, 111–12.

[24] An early text associated with Magdalen School contains several references to boys whose families live elsewhere in England and who board in Oxford to attend the school (Nelson (ed.), *Fifteenth Century School Book*, pp. 13–14 no. 52, pp. 15–18 nos. 55, pp. 60–66, 71). However, it is difficult to distinguish between demies of the college, to whom this would also apply, and boys boarding privately outside the college.

taught anything from 60 to 120 pupils,[25] and Magdalen School is likely to have operated in that range, perhaps at the upper end of it. Waynflete provided a schoolroom large enough to contain at least 100 boys,[26] and a reference to the building in the 1490s claimed that when all the scholars were present there was scarcely a place to sit.[27]

This is not to say that Magdalen College School was the only school in Oxford after 1480. The city needed, and seems to have possessed, facilities for teaching children to read. The ABC is said to have been taught by a master next door to Magdalen School in the 1490s, possibly as an independent venture.[28] In 1548 the king's chantry commissioners were told that Thomas Blauncharde, priest of the Lady chapel in the city church of St Mary Magdalene, 'bryngethe uppe yowthe well', a phrase often used at the time to signify elementary rather than grammar teaching.[29] In a third case, an Oxford chandler named John Langley remembered going to school in about 1552, when he was twelve or so, with the clerk of St Ebbe's church.[30] The assertion of the citizens in 1550 that boys were educated in 'colleges' in the plural is supported by the records of some of the larger foundations. New College maintained a master to instruct its sixteen choristers,[31] and Merton College employed a teacher of grammar in 1490.[32] Wolsey's Cardinal College, during its brief existence from 1525 to 1530, included choristers under the tuition of a grammar master,[33] and a body of choristers remained on the site when Cardinal College was remodelled as King Henry VIII College in the 1530s.[34] In 1549 All Souls College was forbidden to maintain grammar scholars, implying that it had once done so.[35] Some of the houses of monks and friars in the city, too, may have taught children up to the 1530s. We learn by chance that Henry Triplett, an Oxford glover, went 'to school' for about a year in the Dominican Friary in about 1509–10, when he

[25] Orme, *English Schools*, pp. 121–22.

[26] Below, p. 41.

[27] Nelson (ed.), *Fifteenth Century School Book*, p. 39 no. 166.

[28] Ibid., p. 13. This might refer to the college song school for the choristers, but that school was further away, at the Cherwell end of the college (Bloxam, *Register*, I, p. iii).

[29] A.F. Leach, *English Schools at the Reformation, 1546–8* (Westminster, 1896), pt ii, p. 176.

[30] Oxford University Archives (OUA), Chancery Court Depositions, Hyp/B/2, sub anno 1580.

[31] *The Victoria History of the Counties of England* [*VCH*], *Oxfordshire*, III, ed. by H.E. Salter and Mary D. Lobel (London, 1954), 157.

[32] H.E. Salter (ed.), *Registrum Annalium Collegii Mertonensis, 1483–1521*, Oxford Historical Society, 76 (1923), 142.

[33] *Statutes of the Colleges of Oxford*, Cardinal College, II, 13, mentions sixteen choristers and a music master; for the grammar master, see *BRUO* IV, 514 (Richard Sherey).

[34] *VCH Oxfordshire*, III, 235.

[35] Frere and Kennedy (eds), *Visitation Articles and Injunctions*, II, 199.

was fourteen.[36] Still, Magdalen was the most prominent, public, and continuous school in Oxford, and its local importance is confirmed by the city's anxiety to save it.

One other feature of Waynflete's statute of 1480 for Magdalen School ought to be noticed. It provides that 'two or three out of the thirty [demies] at least shall diligently apply themselves to the mysteries of grammar and to verses and the other arts of humanity . . . [so that they] may be able and have power to instruct and inform others also, and have skill and competency for that purpose'.[37] In other words, at least three demies were to learn grammar for its own sake, not merely to qualify them for their university studies. The mysteries of grammar will have meant a detailed understanding of Latin grammar and syntax, while the art of writing verses was considered the most difficult exercise in Latin composition. The pioneer historian of education A.F. Leach interpreted this statute boldly. 'Magdalen was to serve to a certain extent . . . as a Training College for Secondary School teachers.'[38] He pointed to the precedent of William Bingham's foundation at Cambridge, Godshouse, a college later absorbed into Christ's College, which was set up in 1439 to maintain scholars of grammar at university who would learn the subject thoroughly and go on to teach it elsewhere.[39] Waynflete did not make his intentions as clear as Bingham. He may simply have wished the school to provide its own future staff. It is probable (as we shall see) that he had to import his first schoolmaster, John Anwykyll, from outside Oxford, and he must have been familiar with the way in which Winchester College, since his own incumbency, had come to supply its teachers solely from its former pupils. Waynflete may have had a larger vision that his school would train men to teach elsewhere in England, as in the event it did. But if so, his plans were cautious. He arranged for only a small quorum of scholars to pursue this path, and it was probably just one of the ways in which he saw his college upholding religion and learning.

[36] OUA, Hyp/B/2, sub anno 1580.

[37] *Statutes of the Colleges of Oxford*, Magdalen College, II, 16; Ward (ed.), *Statutes of Magdalen College*, p. 23.

[38] Leach, *Schools of Medieval England*, p. 270.

[39] *Early Statutes of Christ's College, Cambridge*, ed. by H. Rackham (Cambridge, 1927), pp. 24–27; Lloyd, *Early History of Christ's College Cambridge*, passim.

The Context of the Foundation

Oxford had been a leading centre of school education in England for 200 years before Waynflete.[40] Indeed, Magdalen College School was founded at the end of Oxford's importance in this respect, not the beginning, and its first 20 years, from 1480 to 1500, were the Indian summer of Oxford's distinction in schooling. Up to the early fifteenth century, Oxford supported more schools than most other towns because of the university. The university taught in Latin, and many scholars who came up intending to follow lectures and read textbooks must have found their knowledge inadequate to do so. There was a thriving market for schoolmasters who would get a man's Latin up to university standard. Such masters were also available to teach boys who were not yet undergraduates but might become so in a few years time. If you were sending a boy away to school, you might as well send him to Oxford — which had good access to most of southern and Midland England — as (say) to Gloucester, Northampton, or Salisbury.

About half a dozen university halls specialized in housing and teaching students of grammar during the fourteenth and fifteenth centuries. There were probably also private-venture schoolmasters. All the teachers of grammar charged fees, and the university levied its tax on them.[41] Some of the teachers were writers as well. We know of a series of Latin grammars by Oxford schoolmasters from the late thirteenth century onwards, and a few of these men and their writings were influential outside Oxford. Obviously, at a national gathering place like Oxford, a teacher's ideas and methods had a better chance of spreading than if he was based in a more provincial town. John Cornwall, a Cornishman who taught in Oxford in the 1340s, was said to have been the first English schoolmaster to use English in the classroom as the language for teaching Latin; previously, French had been used. This innovation, it was claimed, spread from Oxford all over England.[42] John Leland (d. 1428), the chief Oxford schoolmaster of the early fifteenth century, wrote concise textbooks of basic Latin grammar and composition in English which circulated

[40] See R.W. Hunt, 'Oxford Grammar Masters of the Later Middle Ages', *Oxford Studies Presented to Daniel Callus*, Oxford Historical Society, n.s. 16 (1964), 163–93, and David Thomson, 'The Oxford Grammar Masters Revisited', *Mediaeval Studies*, 45 (1983), 298–310.

[41] See A.B. Emden, *An Oxford Hall in Medieval Times* (Oxford, 1927), pp. 173–75, and Thomson, 'Oxford Grammar Masters', pp. 298–310.

[42] Kenneth Sisam (ed.), *Fourteenth Century Verse and Prose* (Oxford, 1955), pp. 148–49.

widely in manuscript copies during the fifteenth century.[43] Within a short space of Leland's death, however, the Oxford grammar schools were experiencing difficulties. By the mid-fifteenth century there were apparently fewer pupils wanting tuition, and hence fewer schoolmasters able to earn a living. By 1470 most of the grammar halls had closed,[44] and 10 years or so later Waynflete apparently had to bring the first recorded schoolmaster of Magdalen, John Anwykyll, to Oxford from elsewhere.[45] It is not certain whether the decline of the fee-paying schools was due to educational, demographic, or other social factors. Certainly Oxford University was less populous in the fifteenth century (as was England), and it was vexed by frequent plagues leading to periodic closures, which may have caused scholars of grammar to study elsewhere. There may have been more competition from free grammar schools, which were becoming more common in England by the 1440s. Whatever the cause, there was apparently a shortage of grammar teachers in Oxford by the 1470s, and Waynflete's school probably represents a deliberate attempt to fill the resulting gap.

He was the first person to endow a free school in Oxford, but he was not the first to do so in England and we need to look at other school foundations in order to understand his. The earliest great endowed free school was Winchester College, founded by William Wykeham in 1382. It provided free education, board, and lodging for seventy scholars who were intended to proceed to Oxford for university education. Winchester was an important foundation but it was not an easy one for anyone else to copy because it was so grand and expensive. Henry VI made it a pattern for Eton College in 1439, but he was the only founder wealthy enough to do so until Wolsey and Henry VIII in the Reformation period. Founders of free schools in the fifteenth century usually copied smaller, cheaper institutions. One of their models was the little grammar school at Wotton-under-Edge (Glos.), established by Lady Katherine Berkeley in 1384. This school was staffed by a single priest-schoolmaster who combined the duty of saying mass for the founder's soul with teaching boys from the neighbourhood free of charge.[46] His salary of about £10 involved an endowment of no more than about £200, which was affordable by gentry or merchant

[43] On Leland, see David Thomson, *A Descriptive Catalogue of Middle English Grammatical Texts* (New York and London, 1979), pp. 6–12, and idem, *An Edition of the Middle English Grammatical Texts* (New York and London, 1984), passim.

[44] Thomson, 'Oxford Grammar Masters Revisited', pp. 303–04.

[45] Below, pp. 15–16.

[46] Discussed by Orme, *English Schools*, pp. 188–89; idem, *Education in the West of England, 1066–1548* (Exeter, 1976), pp. 190–99.

FIG. 2. Waynflete's other grammar school at Wainfleet (Lincs.), containing a chapel above and (probably) schoolroom and master's lodging below. The towers give importance to the building.

founders. A more ambitious plan was to found a chantry college, usually based in a parish church. This maintained several priests to say masses and generally included some clerks and choristers to assist with the music, an almshouse for poor people, and a schoolmaster to teach the choristers and other local pupils. Colleges like this were founded at places like Battlefield (Shropshire) by Roger Ive 1406–09, Higham Ferrers (Northants.) by Archbishop Chichele in 1422, and Westbury-on-Trym (Glos.) by John Carpenter bishop of Worcester 1447–63.[47] They cost more to endow, and were consequently within the reach only of bishops and the lay nobility.

Schools of both kinds began to be founded in significant numbers in the 1440s. This was a time when England was relatively peaceful and prosperous, and the king's own interest in education was spreading to members of his court.

[47] On Battlefield, see *VCH Shropshire*, II, ed. by A.T. Gaydon (London, 1973), 130, and Thomson, *Descriptive Catalogue*, pp. 166–68; on Higham Ferrers, *VCH Northamptonshire*, II, ed. by R.M. Serjeantson and W.R.D. Adkins (London, 1906), 177–79, 218–43; and on Westbury, Orme, *Education in the West of England*, pp. 182–84.

Henry's treasurer Lord Cromwell, for example, founded Tattershall College (Lincs.) after 1439 on the model of the chantry college with school attached. The king's confessor William Alnwick, on the other hand, adopted the framework of the small free-standing school for his foundation at Alnwick (Northumb.) in 1448.[48] Waynflete drew inspiration from both types of schools for his own foundations. Wainfleet, the earlier of the two, was a small grammar school employing a priest, 'if one can readily be had', to celebrate mass and teach grammar (Fig. 2).[49] Magdalen College School resembled the schools of the chantry colleges, although the college to which it was attached was an academic body rather than one solely engaged in worship. Like earlier chantry college schools, it supplied education both to the young members of the institution and to boys and youths who came from outside. It is interesting to note that Magdalen College came to imitate the chantry colleges in another respect: provision for the sick or poor. There is some obscurity about when this function began and whether it was Waynflete's intention, but by the sixteenth century the college provided shelter for up to four persons for three nights, and for longer if necessary.[50]

The three earliest recorded teachers of Magdalen College School — John Anwykyll, John Stanbridge, and John Holt — were three of the first Englishmen whose school textbooks were printed. Because printed books are easier to read than manuscripts and usually survive in larger numbers, historians of education up to the mid-twentieth century were better informed about the work of these masters than about that of fourteenth- and fifteenth-century teachers, whose work survives in manuscript form. Historians were consequently inclined to see the Magdalen College schoolmasters as starting a new era of English education.[51] Not only were they known to be innovative in teaching classical Latin, but their teaching methods were thought to be superior: better structured and more 'user-friendly' to pupils. This is a judgement that requires great care, because the more inflated claims made for the humanist schoolmasters arise from a lack of understanding about previous school education. Ever since the Italian missionaries brought Latin back to England in 597, the English have

[48] Orme, *English Schools*, pp. 200, 202.

[49] *Statutes of the Colleges of Oxford*, Magdalen College, II, 77; Ward (ed.), *Statutes of Magdalen College*, p. 142.

[50] On the poor men of Magdalen College, see H.A. Wilson, *Magdalen College* (London, 1898), pp. 265–66. On colleges and almshouses, see Nicholas Orme and Margaret Webster, *The English Hospital 1070–1570* (New Haven and London, 1995), pp. 143, 285 n. 67.

[51] Notably in Leach, *Schools of Medieval England*, pp. 271–72; Stanier, *Magdalen School*, pp. 26–32; Charlton, *Education in Renaissance England*, p. 106.

found Latin hard to learn. Its grammar and syntax work in such different ways. From about the seventh century onwards, scholars in the British Isles (Irish, Welsh, and English) produced textbooks to teach Latin: textbooks more detailed and sophisticated than those of the Romans themselves.[52] By the fifteenth century there was a long tradition of Latin teaching in England and ingenious methods of doing so had been invented. There were many textbooks: elementary ones in English, like those of John Leland, and advanced ones in Latin for those who had mastered the elements. Some pupils, even in the manuscript age, owned or wrote copies of the texts they used, but much of the teaching assumed that few books were available. Some texts were written in question-and-answer form: the master asked the question and the pupils learnt to give the prescribed answer. Others were composed in Latin verse and were memorized in large amounts, including rules and vocabulary. Pupils were made to argue questions of grammar orally, a good training for logic later on. They also learnt Latin composition, beginning with short sentences and progressing to writing epistolary letters and verses. Finally, they read Latin authors — chiefly Latin religious poetry from the medieval centuries. In short, there was a curriculum, and while it did not produce the same kind of Latinist as did humanist schools later on, it was capable of turning out good scholars or statesmen: a John Wycliffe or a William Waynflete.

A great deal is now known about the fifteenth-century school curriculum both generally and at particular schools. This is because, in about 1400, cheap paper became widely available in England and was adopted for use in schools just as it is today. School notebooks begin to survive after 1400, and these can sometimes be linked to named pupils in known places. They show that, well before the 1480s, masters were using similar techniques to those of Anwykyll, Holt, and Stanbridge later on. Elementary Latin schoolbooks were available in English. Leland, or others inspired by him, had produced a basic *Accidence* teaching Latin morphology, *Comparatio* on the comparison of nouns and adjectives, and *Informacio* and *Formula* which handled syntax and Latin composition.[53] These texts were not only in English; they also gave some recognition to English grammar. They analysed English sentences grammatically and drew the necessary comparisons with Latin usages. There were mnemonic vocabularies in Latin, usually in verse, like *Os facies mentum* which

[52] See Vivien Law, *The Insular Latin Grammarians* (Woodbridge, 1982) and *Grammar and Grammarians in the Early Middle Ages* (London, 1997).

[53] Thomson, *Descriptive Catalogue*, pp. 6–12.

taught the words for the parts of the body and other familiar terms. In school, pupils practised writing Latin prose, often from an English sentence that had to be translated into the other language. The English, it seems, was often set by the master, but sometimes pupils may have composed their own. These English sentences — *vulgaria* as they came to be called — were grammatical exercises, but the material in them had two other purposes. One was to teach wisdom and morality: how to understand life and how to live it. The other purpose was to maintain the pupils' interest and this was done by choosing topics from everyday life. Surviving collections of *vulgaria* are rich in their references to the classroom, the world outside, informal conversation, and even scraps of song and folklore.[54] These are all features of teaching which used to be regarded as innovations of the humanist period; in reality they are much older.

[54] For examples, see Orme, *Education and Society in Medieval and Renaissance England*, chs 5–6, and idem, 'An English Grammar School ca. 1450: Latin Exercises from Exeter (Caius College MS 417/447, folios 16^{v}–24^{v})', *Traditio*, 50 (1995), 261–94.

2. THE EARLY SCHOOLMASTERS AND USHERS

From Anwykyll to Wolsey

The earliest known master of Magdalen College School is John Anwykyll, who is first mentioned as such in the college archives at Michaelmas (29 September) 1483.[55] Little survives about his life or career. He studied grammar at Cambridge University in 1473–74, where he gained permission to graduate as a master of grammar in 1474–75. Cambridge was a centre for training schoolmasters in the fifteenth century — in 1436–42 William Bingham had established his small college of Godshouse to support such training[56] — but Anwykyll may have come from eastern England and have studied at Cambridge merely for convenience. His name is a difficult one to pronounce and his contemporaries found it challenging to write; it survives today in fourteen different spellings. Three of these — Awnwykyll, Alnwekyl, and Allwynkyl — relate to his time at Cambridge.[57] The others arise from his work in Oxford in the 1480s, and here forms like Anwykyll and Anwynkyll predominate, though we also encounter Alwynkyll and Awynkyll.[58] The nearest recorded surname to Anwykyll is Alwinkle, a rare name derived from the parish of Aldwinkle in Northamptonshire.[59] It seems more likely that John's surname was originally Alwinkle, which became Anwykyll in pronunciation, than that it was a different name misunderstood as Alwinkle. The fact that he took a degree in grammar at Cambridge suggests that, like most such graduates, he was already a practising schoolmaster or intended to become one. One of the Cambridge references calls him 'Master' even before he had taken his degree, and this was a title frequently given to schoolmasters by the fifteenth century. Anwykyll was certainly working at Magdalen before Waynflete's death and, in view of the bishop's initiative in founding the school, it is probable that he was William's choice.

In 1483 the Oxford printer Theodoric Rood printed a grammar called *Compendium totius grammatice*, 'a compendium of all grammar', drawing on

[55] MCA, CP 8/49 fol. 16r.

[56] Lloyd, *Christ's College Cambridge*, passim.

[57] S.M. Leathes (ed.), *Grace Book A* (Luard Memorial Series, 1; Cambridge, 1897), pp. 100, 106.

[58] MCA, CP8/49 passim; LCE/1 passim; EL/1 (Ledger A), fols 54v–55r.

[59] J.E. Gover, A. Mawer, and F.M. Stenton, *The Place-Names of Northamptonshire*, English Place-Name Society, 10 (1933), 177–78; *Peterborough Local Administration: Elizabethan Peterborough*, ed. by W.T. Mellows and Daphne H. Gifford, Northamptonshire Record Society, 18 (1956), 24.

the work of the fourth-century Roman grammarian Servius and the fifteenth-century Italian humanist grammarians Lorenzo Valla and Niccolo Perotti.[60] In the same year Rood further published a collection of *Vulgaria*, English and Latin sentences taken or adapted from the plays of Terence, and the way that he printed this text suggests that he meant it to be a companion piece to the *Compendium*.[61] Both works are anonymous, but the *Compendium* begins with two short poems by the Italian humanist Pietro Carmeliano: one naming the author as John and the other praising William Waynflete, to whose suggestion the work is ascribed. The combination of this evidence — Waynflete, 1483, and a master called John — make Anwykyll the likely author of the *Compendium* and consequently of the *Vulgaria*, deductions which have been generally accepted since the late nineteenth century.[62] The *Compendium* contains a few casual references to real people or places: one to St Hugh (of Lincoln), one to Sandwich, two each to Norwich and York, and five to London. Oxford is not mentioned, but there is a discussion of the words 'Magdalenus' and 'Magdalena'.[63] These names, with their bias towards eastern England, are compatible with Anwykyll's Cambridge connection. They suggest that he may have lived in London and even have written the *Compendium* before his arrival in Oxford, but it is difficult to be sure.

The circumstances in which the works were published are also revealing. The *Vulgaria* was printed in an Oxford edition by Rood and in London by William de Machlinia at about the same time, an enterprise unlikely to have been due to Anwykyll alone. Rather, the double publication and Carmeliano's complimentary reference to Waynflete suggest that the bishop was backing Anwykyll's work, reinforcing the impression that the schoolmaster was Waynflete's protégé. But Magdalen too came to think that he was a valuable property. The college bursary books show that he was invited to eat in hall with the fellows from time to time: in Michaelmas term 1485, for example, he dined on the feast of dedication and on two other days.[64] Finally, on 28 June 1487 (the year after

[60] For editions of the work, see A.W. Pollard and G.R. Redgrave (comps), *A Short-Title Catalogue of Books Printed in England . . . 1475–1640*, 2nd edn, ed., rev., and enlarged by W.A. Jackson, F.S. Ferguson, and K.F. Pantzer, 3 vols (London, 1967–91) (hereafter STC), 695–696.7. Citations in the present work are based on the edition issued by Richard Pafraet, Deventer, 1489 (STC 696.1; STC Microfilms, 1126).

[61] STC 23904.

[62] For discussion of this point, see A.H. Brodie, 'Anwykyll's *Vulgaria*: a Pre-Erasmian Textbook', *Neuphilologische Mitteilunge*, 75 (1974), 416–27, esp. p. 418; but Brodie wrote without reference to the documentary sources for Anwykyll.

[63] John Anwykyll, *Compendium totius grammatice* (Oxford, 1483), sig. H1^{r}.

[64] MCA, CP 8/49, fols 41, 48, 50.

Waynflete's death), Magdalen made a contract with Anwykyll to serve the college for 15 years in view of his labour 'concerning a new and very useful form of teaching conceived and composed (*conscriptam*) by him for the school'.[65] This could well be a reference to the *Compendium*. The period of 15 years was conditional on Anwykyll's good behaviour, 'as he has hitherto behaved', and on his willingness to reside in Oxford 'with his wife and family'. During that period, he was to teach grammar, poetry, elegancies of literature, and other humanist learning.[66]

Magdalen's motive in making this contract appears to have been to secure Anwykyll's services for a long time and prevent him from moving to another post. The college was evidently taking its school seriously. At Easter 1486 it had provided Anwykyll with a good deputy in John Stanbridge, a scholar of Winchester and New College, who was already a university BA.[67] It is less clear what Anwykyll gained from his contract. His salary was not increased, but he was promised a college house rent-free in return for repairing the building himself. Perhaps he intended to make extra money by boarding pupils, as many schoolmasters did. The mention of his wife suggests that he was married, another common trait of masters of town schools, but we have no independent knowledge of the wife. Nor is there any record in Magdalen's archives that Anwykyll occupied a college house, although this reflects the very short time that he remained alive. Payments to him by the college ceased at Christmas 1487, and a note in the college records mentions two men teaching in the school thereafter, following 'the death of Master Anwykyll'.[68] He survived his contract by a mere six months.

After Anwykyll's death, Stanbridge remained usher for one term until he was promoted to be master at Easter 1488.[69] By this time, he was called 'Master Stanbridge', having probably graduated MA. Stanbridge was another distinguished man. He had a long career as a teacher and became, after leaving Magdalen, an influential writer of school textbooks.[70] His replacement as usher

[65] Not the 18th, as in Bloxham, *Register*, III, 9.

[66] MCA, EL/1 (Ledger A), fols 54^{v}–55, printed with one or two errors by Bloxam, *Register*, III, 7–9. Bloxam read 'conscriptam' as 'prescriptam', but the 'con' is clear and the word could easily apply to something written by Anwykyll.

[67] Stanbridge resigned his fellowship at New College shortly before 9 April 1486, implying appointment at Magdalen (New College Archives, 946 (Registrum Protocollorum 1455–95), p. 483). For his career, see *BRUO* III, 1754–55.

[68] MCA, LCE/1, fol. 159^{r}.

[69] Ibid., fols 140^{v}, 159^{r}, 161^{v}.

[70] Discussed below, pp. 57, 59–60.

was a man called simply Ashe in the college records, but likely to have been William Ashe, another New College student and therefore a natural choice of deputy for the Wykehamist Stanbridge.[71] Since the time of Bloxam historians have suggested that Stanbridge remained in office until 1494.[72] In fact the financial records listing the masters are deficient between Christmas 1491 when Stanbridge was still in post and Michaelmas 1494 when he had been replaced. He left at an unknown point between these dates, and he had certainly gone by 4 October 1493 when he was admitted as vicar of Bledington in Gloucestershire.[73] This provides us with a clue about his departure. Stanbridge was given the living of Bledington by the abbot and monks of Winchcombe in Gloucestershire, a wealthy Benedictine abbey. The abbot was Richard Kidderminster, a learned man who exerted himself to develop the abbey as a centre of learning.[74] It is easy to imagine him inviting Stanbridge to Winchcombe to be grammar master of the novices or of the non-monastic boys in the abbey, with the promise of a better salary or ecclesiastical promotion. But if so, the arrangement did not last very long. In 1494 Stanbridge left Bledington and moved elsewhere: possibly to the grammar school at Lichfield newly refounded by the local bishop, William Smith. Robert Whittington, who was Stanbridge's pupil, lived in or near Lichfield in the 1490s and this is a likely time and place for them to have met.[75] In 1501 Smith (by then bishop of Lincoln) certainly made Stanbridge master of the hospital of St John at Banbury (Oxon.), with the task of establishing a free grammar school in the building. Stanbridge stayed there as hospital master and schoolmaster until his death in 1510.

When the college accounts resume at Michaelmas 1494, new staff were in office. The master was Andrew Scarbot and his usher was John Holt. Both were masters of arts, both had been fellows of Magdalen, and both were thus the first alumni of the college to hold office. Scarbot, whose surname is that of a kind of

[71] For William Ashe, see *BRUO* I, 55. The usher of Magdalen School dined in New College Hall in 1493 — another pointer to Ashe (New College Archives, 5529 (Liber Senescalli Aulae 1478–99)).

[72] Bloxam, *Register*, III, 19; Beatrice White (ed.), *The Vulgaria of John Stanbridge and the Vulgaria of Robert Whittington*, Early English Text Society, o.s. 187 (1932), p. xvii; Stanier, *Magdalen School*, p. 58; *BRUO* III, 1755.

[73] *BRUO* III, 1755.

[74] W.A. Pantin, 'Abbot Kidderminster and Monastic Studies', *Downside Review*, 47 (1929), 199–211.

[75] Whittington was ordained acolyte in Lichfield Cathedral 28 May 1496 (*The Register of John Morton, Archbishop of Canterbury 1486–1500*, ed. by C. Harper-Bill, II, Canterbury and York Society, 78 (1991), 116). His acknowledgement of Stanbridge as his former *praeceptor* occurs in Whittington's *Syntaxis* (London, 1521, STC 25548), sig. A1v.

beetle (compare the word 'scarab'), came from Bury St Edmunds.[76] He was the youngest son of a prosperous burgess of the town who died when Andrew was about seven, leaving him a small piece of property there.[77] By 1494 he was also a priest. Scarbot has not attracted the attention of historians, but he evidently had a vocation to teach. He remained in office until 1499 and, as we shall see, he can be linked with one of the well-known schoolbooks used at the school in this period.[78] Holt, too, came from a wealthy urban family (in his case Chichester) and was ordained as a priest. His career as a schoolmaster was more brilliant than Scarbot's.[79] Even as usher he won golden opinions for his teaching from the president of Magdalen, Richard Mayew, since the college accounts for Michaelmas term 1495 record a bonus of 13*s.* 4*d.* 'paid to him, by commandment of the president, for his diligence over the scholars in the grammar school'.[80] Shortly afterwards, at Easter 1496, Holt resigned to become schoolmaster in the household of John Morton, archbishop of Canterbury, at Lambeth Palace.[81] From there Holt wrote a complimentary letter to Mayew, who may well have recommended him to Morton. It was probably at Lambeth that he came to know the young Thomas More, and certainly there that he wrote (at Morton's suggestion) an elementary Latin grammar *Lac Puerorum.* From Morton's employment, Holt went first to be master of Chichester School and finally teacher of grammar to Prince Henry, later Henry VIII. He acquired two wealthy benefices as well as his paid work as schoolmaster, ending his career with a net income of some £40 a year — unusually high for a teacher. Both Scarbot and Holt died in their early thirties. Scarbot disappears from the college accounts at Easter 1499: probably through death, because no later mentions of him have been found. Holt died in 1504, perhaps on the threshold of a distinguished career in the Church; the teacher of a future king would have been well-placed for advancement.

Because Scarbot departed or died at Easter 1499 in the middle of the academic session, there was need for an immediate replacement. That was found in

[76] For his biography, see *BRUO* III, 1651.

[77] Bury St Edmunds, Suffolk Record Office, IC 500/2/2 (Hawlee, 189). I am indebted to Dr Peter Northeast for this information.

[78] Below, pp. 34–5.

[79] See *BRUO* II, 953–54, and Nicholas Orme, 'John Holt (d. 1504), Tudor Schoolmaster and Grammarian', *The Library*, 6th ser. 18 (1996), 283–305.

[80] MCA, LCE/2, fol. 24ʳ.

[81] Ibid., fols 37ᵛ–38ʳ records payments to Holt and another usher called Howell for the three terms from Michaelmas 1495 to Midsummer 1496. Commons was paid to one of them for one term. This shows that Holt (who was not paid commons) taught for two terms till Easter, and Howell during the third term.

FIG. 3. Thomas Wolsey, briefly master of Magdalen College School in 1499: a drawing based on a lost portrait of him as a younger man.

Thomas Wolsey, another college fellow and the most famous of all Magdalen's early teachers (Fig. 3). It is likely that Wolsey helped out as a locum rather than taking up office as a long-term commitment. He led the school for only two terms and left at Michaelmas 1499 when another master, probably Richard Jackson, was found. A.B. Emden thought that Wolsey ran the school between September 1498 and Easter 1499.[82] He may have thought so because of the story that the future cardinal acted as guardian and schoolmaster to the three sons of the marquess of Dorset who were then staying at Magdalen. The marquess is said to have invited Wolsey and the boys to come home for Christmas. Then, impressed by the results of Wolsey's teaching, he rewarded him with a rectory in Somerset, which started his career in the Church.[83] This story was told a long time afterwards by George Cavendish in his *Life of Wolsey*, written in the 1550s, but the college accounts do not quite bear it out. In the financial year from Michaelmas 1498 to 1499, they record payments to Scarbot for two terms and Wolsey for two.[84] It is more likely that these terms were consecutive than alternating, so that if Wolsey spent Christmas 1498 with the marquess, he did so as the boys' guardian rather than as their schoolmaster. Still, Wolsey's later life shows that he had an interest in grammar schools. In the 1520s, he set out to incorporate Ipswich school, the local grammar school of his home town, into a great new college on the lines of Eton or Winchester, though the project collapsed when he fell from power. He attached his name to a school grammar textbook, and seems to have thought of imposing a uniform system of grammar on every English school.[85] These interests may owe something to his time at Magdalen, and suggest that his two terms of teaching in the school were not without an influence on the rest of his life.

The Masters and Ushers: An Analysis

It would take too long to consider all the pre-Reformation schoolmasters individually, so let us examine them as a group.[86] Fourteen masters and thirty-one ushers are known to have ruled the school between 1480 and 1540, and as three ushers were promoted to be masters, the total reaches forty-two men altogether. What we know of their careers falls roughly into three categories:

[82] *BRUO* III, 2077.

[83] George Cavendish, *The Life and Death of Cardinal Wolsey*, ed. by R.S. Sylvester, Early English Text Society, o.s. 243 (1959), 5; for the date of the *Life*, see pp. xxvi–xxvii.

[84] MCA, LCE/2, fol. 91^{v}.

[85] Below, p. 64.

[86] The following discussion is based on the revised list of masters and ushers (below, pp. 68–71) and on their biographies in *BRUO* I–IV.

their previous histories including the qualifications they possessed when they arrived at the school, their spans of office, and what they did afterwards. Most were young men, frequently in their early twenties. John Hynde (by 1524) and John Stokesley (1496) were about twenty-two when appointed, Wolsey (1499) about twenty-five, Stanbridge (by 1486) not more than about twenty-five, Richard Jackson (1499) about twenty-six, and Scarbot (by 1494) not more than about twenty-seven. At least four had probably or certainly taught in other schools: Anwykyll (by 1483) somewhere unknown, Thomas Brinknell (by 1502) at Wainfleet, Thomas Stanbridge (1517) at Banbury, and Richard Sherrey (1532) at Cardinal College Oxford. Most, however, had no experience of schoolrooms other than as pupils. They lived in an age when learning a subject was reckoned to qualify a person to teach it. About half were graduates when they came, of whom eight are recorded as MAs, ten as BAs, and two as holders of degrees in grammar. Another four gained degrees during their tenure, and some of the BAs graduated as MAs. Several other masters and ushers are not recorded as graduating, especially the ushers, and may never have done so. Nine masters were priests when they arrived or seem to have been ordained while in office. Many others, in contrast, were not yet priests, either because they had not reached the statutory age of twenty-four or had not decided to commit themselves to taking a vow of celibacy. These non-priests can be regarded as clergy in that Magdalen College was a kind of religious house. They may have held minor clerical orders (the so-called first tonsure), and would certainly have claimed to be clergy if they had been charged with a crime in court. Equally, they can be seen as laymen because they were free to marry and take up lay careers. They might regard themselves as having a freer life than that of priests, with more licence for pleasure or lawlessness. And at least one besides Anwykyll, John Hynde, was married while he was schoolmaster.[87]

Next, we may consider their lengths of time in office. If we divide the period 1480 to 1540 by the number of staff, we get an average tenure of about 4.3 years per master and 2 years per usher. These figures reflect the fact that a few of the staff, like Wolsey, were probably doing temporary duty until a permanent teacher could be appointed; the average tenures of the permanent staff were a little higher. Teachers at other leading schools held office for roughly similar periods. At Eton College fourteen schoolmasters held office between 1479 and 1534 with an average tenure of about 4 years, and twenty-three known ushers

[87] *BRUO* IV, 311.

taught between 1480 and 1540, averaging about 2.6 years.[88] At Winchester College there were nine masters between 1484 and 1541, with an average tenure of about 6 years, and thirteen ushers between 1475 and 1543, with an average of about 5.2 years.[89] Why were terms of office relatively short? Most schools attracted some professional teachers like Stanbridge, who taught throughout their careers. There were various reasons, however, why others stayed only briefly. A few masters died in office, such as Anwykyll and Scarbot. Occasionally, one might be dismissed as unsatisfactory, though this is not recorded at Magdalen. Most commonly, masters left for other work. A well-reputed man might be offered a better paid job, as was apparently the case with Stanbridge and certainly Holt. Equally, teaching was a path to other employment rather than an end in itself. It offered support for a year or two before ordination or presentation to a benefice. At Magdalen in particular, it held out the possibility of gaining patronage from the college or its friends, resulting in the grant of a Church post.

Of our forty-two men, about twenty-six had further known careers. Of these, at least nine became schoolmasters elsewhere — a process we shall examine later. A greater number preferred to build careers as clergy, for whom openings were more numerous and possibilities of promotion better than in schools. At least eighteen of the forty-two can be shown to have held Church benefices, including Birchynshaw, Goldyve, Holt, and Stanbridge, who combined such posts with teaching. Of the rest in this category, ten became parish clergy as rectors or vicars, and two (Fryer and Robertson) gained cathedral canonries. Two rose to be bishops — Wolsey at York and John Stokesley at London — but both of these taught in the school only briefly. Even in the early sixteenth century it was not much easier for schoolmasters to rise in the Church than it had been in Waynflete's time.[90]

[88] Sir Wasey Sterry, *The Eton College Register, 1441–1698* (Eton, 1943), pp. xxxii–xxxiii.

[89] The masters at Winchester are listed in Kirby, *Winchester Scholars*, passim, and the ushers by H.F. Chitty, 'The Second Masters of Winchester College', *The Wykehamist*, no. 551 (April 1916), pp. 2–3.

[90] Orme, *Education and Society*, pp. 58–59.

FIG. 4. An early nineteenth-century engraving of Magdalen College School. The original schoolroom is on the ground floor; the upper stories have been remodelled to incorporate the chapel of Magdalen Hall.

FIG. 5. The south elevation of Magdalen College School as it appeared in 1820, traced by J.C. Buckler in 1850.

FIG. 6. Another view of the south elevation as it was in 1829, traced by Buckler in 1849. Magdalen Hall is on the left; the gate on the right leads to the lane between the school and the college.

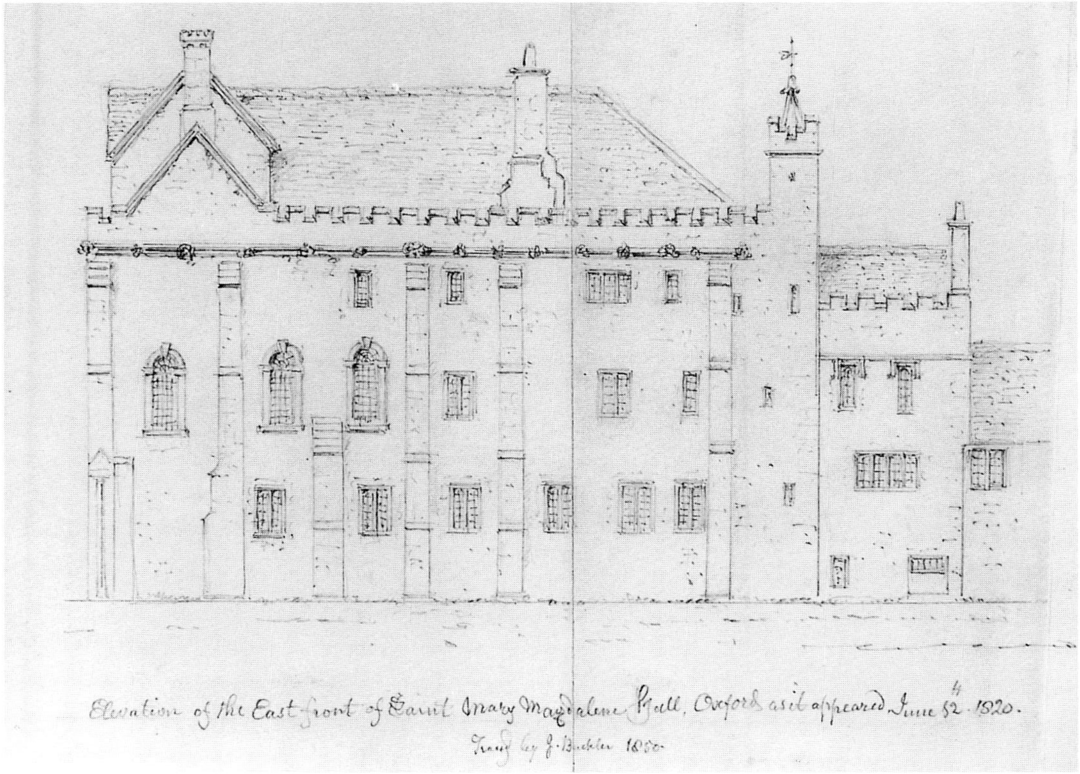

FIG. 7. The east elevation of the school as it existed in 1820, traced by Buckler in 1850.

FIG. 8. Another nineteenth-century drawing of the east elevation of the school, showing the college wall and gate.

FIG. 9. The west elevation of the school as it appeared in 1827, drawn by Buckler. At this time the south range of Magdalen Hall still stood to the west of the school; the rest of the hall had been destroyed.

FIG. 10. The interior of the schoolroom facing north, drawn by Buckler in 1849. It was then partly panelled and contained long forms with a desk in front of each one. The chief object was the master's desk, backed by an ornate carving in the Renaissance style.

Fig. 11. An engraving of the schoolroom facing south, as it was in 1828. The usher's desk, less ornate than the master's, is placed beside the school entrance.

3. THE LIFE AND WORK OF THE SCHOOL

The Study of Latin

Studying masters' careers is one way of judging the quality of teaching in early Tudor schools. Much more can be learnt, however, from the textbooks in use and the work of the pupils, when these survive, and the historian of Magdalen College School is fortunate to possess three sources of this kind from the period between the 1480s and the 1520s. The earliest is John Anwykyll's *Compendium totius grammatice*, first printed in 1483, with its appended *Vulgaria* taken from Terence. These are the only works attributed to an early master of the school to be published while he was master, and it is a reasonable assumption that they embody his own teaching programme. The contract by which the college renewed his appointment in 1487 suggests as much when it praises the 'form of teaching that he has composed'.[91] The second source is Arundel MS 249 in the British Library. This is a manuscript collection of school texts probably made by a member of Magdalen College in about 1504, since it includes letters referring to President Mayew (1480–1508) and to other people connected with the college. Its contents are also likely to reflect the work of the Magdalen classroom, especially a set of *vulgaria* for teaching the composition of Latin, well known since they were edited by the late William Nelson in 1956.[92] The third source, likewise in the British Library, is Royal MS 12.B.xx. This is a group of five manuscript and printed texts, bound up together without any common indication of their origin. One of the manuscripts is a further collection of *vulgaria*, and this (as we shall see) bears signs of having been composed at Magdalen.[93]

The two sets of *vulgaria* are an important part of this evidence. They are passages of English prose with Latin translations and, like earlier *vulgaria*, make frequent allusions to the school in which they were used. The Arundel *vulgaria* consist of 387 passages in both Latin and English versions, which mention Oxford, the study of grammar, and boys going on to undergraduate studies. Their preservation in a miscellany with Magdalen connections points to their origin in Magdalen College School. The Royal *vulgaria* contain only

[91] MCA, EL/1 (Ledger A), fols 54^{v}–55; Bloxam, *Register*, III, 7–9, and above, nn. 65–66.

[92] Nelson (ed.), *Fifteenth Century School Book*.

[93] Printed in Nicholas Orme, 'An Early-Tudor Oxford Schoolbook', *Renaissance Quarterly*, 34 (1981), 11–39, reprinted in Orme, *Education and Society*, pp. 123–51.

eighty-eight passages, but the latter part of the text is missing so the original span is unknown. They refer to Oxford, to grammar schooling, and to a college environment; they resemble the Arundel *vulgaria* in character, and four of the Arundel passages appear in similar (but not identical) form in the Royal manuscript. The Magdalen context of the Royal *vulgaria* is therefore another reasonable assumption. Details of the authorship and date of the two works, on the other hand, are more difficult to establish. Neither set has an author's name attached to it, and the Royal *vulgaria* are additionally hard to date although they are likely to belong to the years 1512–14 or possibly 1522–27.[94] The Arundel *vulgaria* have the advantage of containing three references to historical events. One mentions the embargo on trade between England and the Netherlands imposed by Henry VII on 18 September 1493 and lifted on 28 February 1496.[95] Another notes that wheat, peas, and corn are being sold cheaper than they have been in human memory. Grain was cheap in both 1495–96 and in 1499–1500, but the former years must be meant because of the emphasis on the novelty of the situation.[96] The third allusion is to the taking down and replacement of the weathercock of St Paul's Cathedral, which was carried out between December 1497 and May 1498.[97]

Nelson deserves the credit for identifying all three of these events in the Arundel *vulgaria*. Unfortunately, he postdated the last of them by one year to 1498–99 through a confusion in his source.[98] He also failed to notice a further chronological indicator. The Arundel *vulgaria* contain three mentions of the plague, but they do not speak about any public consequences of it: the interruption of academic life, the dispersal of scholars from Oxford, or the evacuation of the college community to one of its rural manors.[99] The Royal *vulgaria*, in contrast, betray a stronger fear of the plague and allude to both the suspension of studies and the withdrawal of scholars to the countryside.[100] Now, the best series of data on the plague in Oxford, the records of Merton College, suggest that there were four serious outbreaks from 1486 to 1493 and

[94] Orme, *Education and Society*, p. 126.

[95] Nelson (ed.), *Fifteenth Century School Book*, p. 91 no. 379; Paul L. Hughes and James F. Larkin (eds), *Tudor Royal Proclamations*, 3 vols (New Haven, 1964–69), I, 35, 37.

[96] Nelson (ed.), *A Fifteenth Century School Book*, p. 92 no. 382; J.E. Thorold Rogers, *A History of Agriculture and Prices in England*, 6 vols (Oxford, 1866–87), IV, 248–49.

[97] Nelson (ed.), *A Fifteenth Century School Book*, p. 93, no. 386; A.H. Thomas and I.D. Thornley (eds), *The Great Chronicle of London*, (London, 1938; repr. Gloucester, 1983), p. 286.

[98] Nelson (ed.), *A Fifteenth Century School Book*, p. 100.

[99] Ibid., p. 45 no. 196, p. 83 no. 349, p. 87 no. 364.

[100] Orme, *Education and Society*, p. 137 nos 22–23, p. 140 no. 36, p. 143 no. 55, p. 147 no. 78.

several others after 1501, but mention none between 1493 and 1501.[101] This further suggests that the Arundel *vulgaria* were written during that period. Because of the connections between the Arundel manuscript and Magdalen College, Nelson reasonably assumed that its *vulgaria* were the work of one of the college schoolmasters. His misdating of the weathercock reference, however, made it necessary for him to find a man in office from September 1493 to May 1499, and no master's period of tenure appeared to last for so long. Perhaps for this reason, Nelson put forward no name for the author, and left open the field for other suggestions. Stanier, in 1958, proposed Holt without giving reasons for saying so.[102] Emden, in 1959, nominated Stanbridge on the grounds that the *vulgaria* mention Winchester College and that Stanbridge was the only early Magdalen schoolmaster who had studied at Winchester.[103]

Neither proposal is very convincing. There is but one brief reference to Winchester College as a place where grammar is taught, a fact well known to anyone at the time.[104] Stanbridge, as we have seen, had departed from Magdalen by October 1493 and Holt did so at Easter 1496. If either wrote the *vulgaria*, we would have to explain why his exercises went on referring to his old environment after he left it, rather than to his new one. The Arundel *vulgaria* reveal no special knowledge of London (Holt's destination), and none of places with which Stanbridge might have been connected. A better explanation is that the work belongs to the mastership of Andrew Scarbot. Scarbot, as has been shown, did not necessarily begin his reign in 1494. Stanbridge had left at least twelve months before, perhaps earlier, so that Scarbot's tenure can be conjectured back to at least the autumn of 1493. He remained as master until Easter 1499. The weathercock evidence, correctly located no later than May 1498, is therefore compatible with his tenure; so is the grain reference, and the trade embargo could be, as it began but a year before his first known appearance as master and at a time when Stanbridge must have been leaving, if not already gone. It looks, in consequence, as if the Arundel *vulgaria* belong to Scarbot's tenure of the school and reflect his teaching. He may have written them himself but, as with all *vulgaria*, it is possible that they partly represent work done by

[101] Salter (ed.), *Registrum*, pp. 92, 100, 124, 172–73, 253, 283, 338, 392, 428, 478. This evidence is not contradicted by the more slender records of Magdalen: Macray, *Register*, I, 16–33, passim.

[102] Stanier, *Magdalen School*, p. 34: perhaps because the Arundel MS contains one letter to Holt and one possibly by him.

[103] Emden, *BRUO* III, 1755.

[104] Nelson (ed.), *Fifteenth Century School Book*, p. 23 no. 94.

his predecessors, assistants, or pupils. They are, however, more plausibly connected with his name and his tenure than with anyone else's.

Let us now turn from the sources to the evidence they contain. The Arundel manuscript suggests that Magdalen School in the 1490s studied a range of grammatical works and topics that did not differ greatly from those used in earlier fifteenth-century schools. It contains part of a version of the text *Sum, es, fui*, an English work on the forms of the verbs *esse*, *ferre*, and their compounds, which was the kind of elementary grammar popular since the time of John Leland (fols 118^{r}–120^{v}). Other works in the manuscript include a Latin vocabulary in verse (fols 88^{r}–90^{v}), a Latin–English word list arranged in topics (fols 92^{r}–93^{v}), short phrases and *vulgaria* in English and Latin (fols 62^{r}–72^{v}), the longer *vulgaria* passages edited by Nelson (fols 9^{r}–61^{r}), and a collection of bilingual model letters (fols 73^{r}–80^{v}). There are also twenty real letters, probably intended as models too because many of the names in them have been omitted or reduced to initials (fols 81^{r}–87^{r}). Collectively these items cannot represent the whole of the school's curriculum, but they cover significant parts of it and indicate that, at its elementary stages, it involved the teaching (in the accustomed ways) of basic grammar, vocabulary, and the writing of Latin prose sentences and letters. Although the Arundel and Royal manuscripts include *vulgaria* which are mostly longer and more elaborate than most fifteenth-century examples, it would be unwise to say that these represent an improvement of work in schools. Arundel contains short phrases too, and the longer passages probably reflect the fact that they were used with pupils in their mid- or late teens who were going on to higher university studies.

Anwykyll's *Compendium*, too, is a more advanced work. It is almost wholly written in Latin and was therefore suitable only for pupils who had made some progress in the language. Its four parts handle Latin spelling, grammar, pronunciation, and syntax, omitting the basic forms of the parts of speech but dealing with more complex words and phrases. The teaching methods of the book are conservative. At times it is framed as a series of questions and answers in prose; at times it expounds its points with examples of short Latin sentences, and on rare occasions with English *vulgaria*.[105] Each section of prose material is followed by Latin verses which repeat what has been said in a form that could be memorized. These features are all found in earlier grammars in England. The novelty of the book lay in the fact that it drew on the classical grammarian Servius and the Italian humanist grammarians Valla and Perotti, and like them

[105] E.g. Anwykyll, *Compendium*, sigs. E5^{r}, I1, I4^{r}, M2^{v}.

adopted classical Latin authors as its models. It cites, for example, Cicero's *Epistolae*, Horace's *Ars Poetica* and *Satires*, Juvenal's *Satires*, Sallust, Terence's *Eunuchus*, *Adelphoe*, and *Phormio*, and Virgil's *Bucolics*, *Georgics*, and *Aeneid*. There are a few references to medieval authorities including Albertus Magnus, Hugutio, the Psalms, and the *Catholicon* of Johannes Januensis, but these are infrequent compared with the classical citations. Albertus and the rest receive far less attention than in fourteenth- and earlier fifteenth-century grammars. It does not follow, however, that Anwykyll's class was yet reading all these classical authors. We can be certain only that the schoolmaster knew about them and wanted his pupils to respect them.

The three sets of *vulgaria* — the Terence ones and those of the Arundel and Royal manuscripts — also follow a traditional method. Boys were apparently given such sentences or passages in the English versions and turned them into Latin, the Latin version supplying a model against which the pupil's effort could be checked. The novelty of the *vulgaria* based on Terence lay, like that of the *Compendium*, in the taking of a classical author as the literary standard.[106] *Vulgaria* in fifteenth-century schools often centred on teaching an informal, colloquial style, and Anwykyll acted shrewdly in choosing an author like Terence who wrote in that way. Some of the sentences from Terence convey wise and moral advice while others refer to everyday life and conversation — both well-established themes in *vulgaria* writing. The fact that the Terence *vulgaria* were issued in at least six printed editions, the last as late as 1529, shows that Anwykyll judged correctly what schools required.[107] The Arundel and Royal *vulgaria*, especially the latter, are more ornate in style but convey a similar mixture of virtuous teachings and matters of daily experience. As they do not usually refer to classical authors overtly, it would take a good deal of research to establish their debt in this respect. The Arundel *vulgaria* contain only four clear references to classical Latin writers — one each to Cicero's *De Amicitia* and *De Officiis*, Ovid's *Amores*, and Terence's *Andria*[108] — with other

[106] Of about 530 sentences and phrases in the work, it is possible to locate 361 in particular places in six of Terence's plays (Brodie, 'Anwykyll's *Vulgaria*', p. 422).

[107] Below, p. 58.

[108] Nelson (ed.), *Fifteenth Century School Book*, p. 44 no. 192, p. 64 no. 272, p. 83 nos 346 and 348, pp. 86–87 no. 363.

possible allusions to Sallust's *Catilina* and Livy's *Ab Urbe Condita Libri*.[109] The classical context is a little stronger in the Royal *vulgaria*, which for that reason alone may be later in date. Its fewer passages include eleven identifiable references to classical authors and to a wider range of their works. These include Cicero's *De Divinatio*, his *Orator* (twice), Horace's *Ars Poetica* (twice), his *Epistles*, Martial's *Epigrams*, Ovid's *Heroides*, Sallust's *Catilina*, Terence's *Adelphoe*, and an unspecified text of Virgil.[110]

Altogether, the evidence of the texts used in Magdalen College School suggests that the influence of humanist Latin developed gradually in the classroom, perhaps over a couple of decades, rather than immediately and completely. Anwykyll did not entirely turn his back on medieval grammar and its authorities; nor, perhaps, did his earliest successors. It may be significant that Stanbridge's innovations as a grammarian were published during his time at Banbury in the early 1500s, rather than at Magdalen a decade earlier. In Scarbot's regime, too, there seems to have been some hesitation between late medieval and humanist usages, with sympathy still for the former. One revealing passage in the Arundel *vulgaria* reflects that

> Ther is so great diversite of autors of gramer and of eloquence that I cannot tell to whom I may inclyne, for theis new auctors doth rebuke the noble deeds of them that ben before them; therfor oure mindes be plukkyde by ther and thither, but we be so variable and wandrynge of mynde that we covett the newer thynges and tho thei be worse.[111]

These words come not from a school run by a man who had grown old in traditional ways, but from one whose master may well have been taught by Anwykyll in the new style and who died in his early thirties!

The School Building

People today will wish to know about the social history of a Tudor school as well as its curriculum. What was the building like, what kinds of pupils studied there, and what were the arrangements for the timetable, holidays, and discipline? The site of the building is easy to establish because it was the same

[109] Ibid., p. 4 no. 9, p. 64 no. 273. The names Sulpice and Symprony on p. 70 no. 292 may be drawn from Livy, *Ab Urbe Condita Libri*, IX, 45; X, 9. Other allusions to Roman history which are said to have come from 'the chronicles' (ibid., pp. 64–66 nos 274, 276, 277) could have been taken from late medieval chronicles, e.g. *Polychronicon Ranulphi Higden*, ed. by C. Babington and J.R. Lumby, 9 vols (London, Rolls Series, 1865–68), IV, 54–55 (Hannibal), 150–204 (Pompey) and 200–01 (Mennius Cato). The latter source does not, however, mention Hannibal's use of fire and vinegar when crossing the Alps, which is in Livy's account (*Ab Urbe Condita Libri*, XXI, 37).

[110] Orme, *Education and Society*, pp. 149–51.

[111] Nelson (ed.), *Fifteenth Century School Book*, pp. 19–20 no. 78.

from 1480 until 1828. It stood to the west of the college, separated by a lane from the castellated wall which used to form the west side of the front or 'St John's' quadrangle of Magdalen College. The school's north wall lay approximately where the south wall of the present Grammar Hall stands, and the building stretched some seventy feet south of that. The ground between the college wall and Longwall Street belonged to Magdalen College and contained, when the college was founded, a row of houses.[112] It is likely that the easternmost of these was demolished to make way for the school building, which shows every sign of having been a new one. West of the school by 1480 there was another house called 'Gramerhalle', rented from the college by a master of arts.[113] This seems to have been the nucleus of what became Magdalen Hall, an official hall of the university governed by a principal. The name 'Gramerhalle' raises the question whether the house at first accommodated private students attending the grammar school, and that may well have been the case. Eventually, however, Magdalen Hall became a community of undergraduates studying the university arts course, and had little connection with the school other than sharing its site.

Reconstructing the features of the school, as Waynflete built it, is a difficult task. The structure was much altered in later times, and virtually all of it was demolished in 1828. The earliest evidence is to be found in a drawing of Magdalen College made by John Bereblock in 1566, one of thirteen views of university buildings which he exhibited in St Mary's church at the visit of Queen Elizabeth in that year (Fig. 12).[114] His college drawings do not usually contain extraneous buildings, and the inclusion of the school may be significant. Only a short time previously the college and the city had exerted themselves to defend the school from the commissioner of the queen's brother Edward VI. By featuring it in his drawing, Bereblock may have wished to affirm its continuing importance to Oxford and to the university. He shows it as a short, wide structure of two storeys, viewed from the south-west. The south side, facing High Street, has a large double door on the lower right-hand side, with one window beside it and three above. The west wall is unbuttressed and contains windows on each floor. The parapets of the walls are castellated, like the

[112] On the early history of this area, see Brian Durham *et al.*, 'The Infirmary and Hall of the Medieval Hospital of St. John the Baptist at Oxford', *Oxoniensia*, 56 (1991), 22–23.

[113] MCA, EP/48/2.

[114] Oxford, Bodleian Library, MS Bodley 13, fol. 8^{v}, reproduced in Catto and Evans (eds), *Late Medieval Oxford*, fig. 4(l).

FIG. 12. John Bereblock's drawing of Magdalen College School in 1566, showing the south entrance door and window, the turret and the west wall of the college with a postern gate. The details of the school building, however, appear to be a mirror image of their real locations.

college, and there is a shallow gable on the south side, accompanied by a low-pitched roof with two chimneys. At the north-west corner of the roof stands a rectangular turret, topped by a crocketed spire, providing access to the tiles. By the south-east corner of the school, a small postern gate gives entry through the college wall into St John's quadrangle.

Bereblock's picture is worth attention because it dates from a time before many changes had been made to the building. Unfortunately, it is not very accurate — a fact that can be established from depictions of the school in the 1820s, just before it was destroyed. Several drawings of the building were made between 1820 and 1828, and were later copied by the architectural historian J.C. Buckler in 1849–50.[115] They survive in the college archives, along with one or two prints of the school from the early nineteenth century, and are larger and more convincing than Bereblock's work.[116] The drawings are detailed enough to enable original features of the structure to be distinguished from later ones, and their relevance extends beyond Magdalen School. Few school buildings earlier than the Reformation remain today, and the Magdalen drawings are a valuable addition to the evidence. They suggest that the lower south frontage of the school was the exterior part least changed from Waynflete's time. The original entrance doorway still stood on the ground floor, somewhat to the left of the centre, not to the right as in Bereblock, and was narrower than he suggests. It was arched in the perpendicular style, and had a small two-light window above it with a dripmould and foliated heads to the lights. A slightly larger similar window stood a little lower down to the right of the door. The schoolroom occupied the whole ground floor and had five windows on each side, not symmetrically placed. By Buckler's time, these windows had lost any external features typical of Waynflete's period. The east and west sides of the building were supported by buttresses, and a turret (presumably containing a staircase) stood towards the north-east corner of the building — not the north-west where Bereblock located it. It looks indeed as if he transposed the positions of the turret, school doorway, and lower south-facing window.

Unlike the ground-floor schoolroom, which seems to have survived relatively well, the upper parts of Waynflete's building had been much remodelled by the 1820s. The original first floor probably contained accommodation for the master and usher, but at a later date the south end of this floor was made into a chapel for the adjoining community of Magdalen Hall, resulting in the insertion of new round-headed windows. An attic storey was added in place of the original roof, and the building was extended on the north side of the turret with a small extra block. This block was spared when the school building was demolished in the 1820s and still exists today as the 'Grammar Hall' in Magdalen College. The turret remains too, and is therefore the only visible vestige of Waynflete's school. Its position, however, has been reversed: it now fronts a building whereas originally it backed one. A further feature worth

[115] Buckler was the author of *Observations on the Original Architecture of Saint Mary Magdalen College, Oxford* (London, 1823); this contains references to the school buildings on pp. 18–21.

[116] MCA, MS 881 (v): Bloxam's interleaved copy of vol. III of his *Register of Magdalen College*. A further engraving of the school is preserved in Edward Chapman's 'Views of Old Oxford', I, 5 *supra*, also in the college archives.

mentioning is a large arched gateway between the south-east corner of the school and the west wall of St John's quadrangle. The gateway led to the lane alongside the east wall of the school, allowing access to the innermost grounds of the college (Fig. 13).

The inside of the schoolroom is depicted in one of Buckler's drawings and in an undated engraving of about the same period (Fig. 14). At that time it measured 72 feet by 24 feet 9 inches internally, and this is likely to have been the original shape or close to it. Long narrow schoolrooms are found elsewhere in the fifteenth and early sixteenth centuries.[117] One existed at Eton, where Waynflete had been involved with the foundation: 76 feet by 24 feet. The school building at Wainfleet (and therefore perhaps the schoolroom there) was 70 feet by 20 internally,[118] and the schoolroom at Berkhampstead (Herts.), founded in the 1540s, was 70 by 27. The nineteenth-century pictures show the ceiling of Magdalen School supported by two rows of six wooden posts. A large wooden desk with ornamental panelling behind it stood against the centre of the north wall, probably for the master. This desk was built in the Elizabethan or Jacobean periods, to judge from the style. A similar but smaller desk stood on the south wall beside the entrance and would have served appropriately for the usher, whose name (from the Latin *hostiarius*) means 'door keeper'. Long benches were arranged around the walls, leaving the centre of the room open. Although this is the layout of later times, the original one may not have been vastly different. It is likely that Anwykyll and his successors had a large panelled seat (similar seats are shown in early schoolbooks),[119] and that there were forms or benches for the pupils. Waynflete's contract for building Wainfleet School included provision for 'desks and all things necessary to carpentry work for a chapel and schoolhouse'.[120] There is one reference in the Royal *vulgaria* to pupils pinning up Latin verses on a post, which may well apply to one of those in the schoolroom.[121] The placing of the windows fairly high and the presence of the college wall near the east side meant that light was admitted rather than external distractions. A long narrow schoolroom allowed the master and usher, from their seats, to keep an eye on every boy. It enabled the school to be subdivided for purposes of work: both into two halves and, more precisely, into

117 On school buildings and furnishings in this period, see Malcolm Seaborne, *The English School: Its Architecture and Organization 1370–1870* (London, 1971), pp. 1–17.

118 MCA, Deeds, Candlesby 16; William Chandler, *The Life of William Waynflete* (London, 1811), pp. 367–70.

119 Below, p. 62.

120 MCA, Deeds, Candlesby 16, printed in Chandler, *Life of William Waynflete*, pp. 367–70.

121 Orme, *Education and Society*, p. 146.

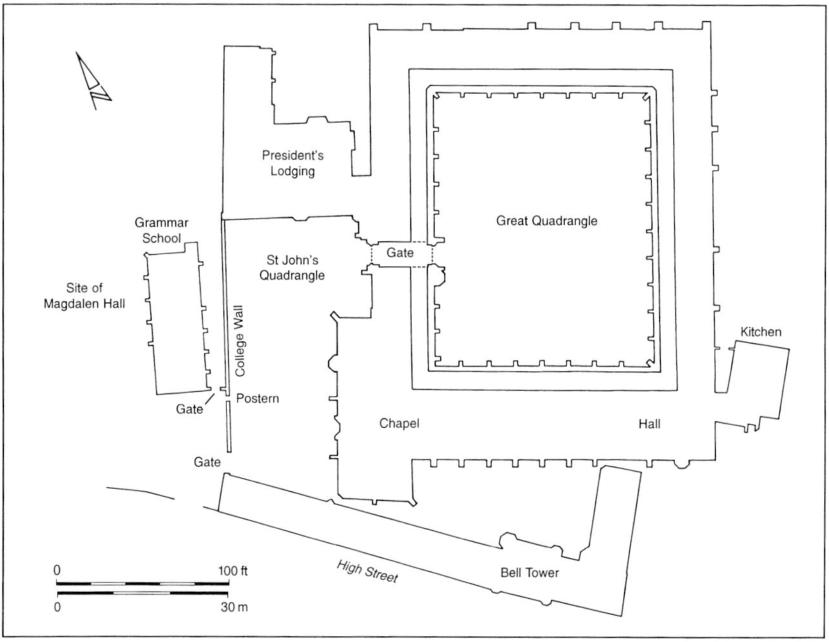

FIG. 13. The college school in relation to the other early buildings of the college.

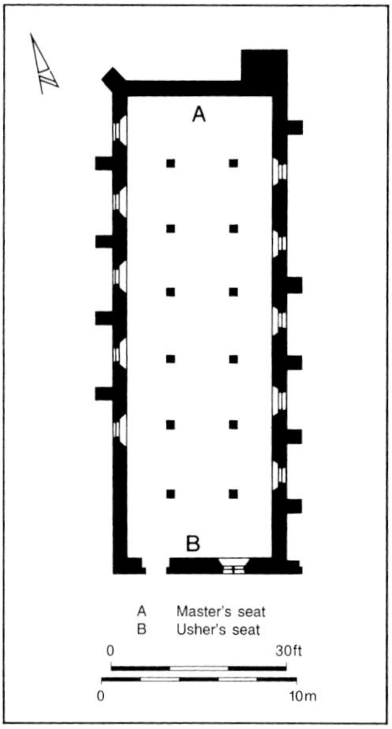

FIG. 14. The schoolroom, based on Buckler's research when the room still existed in the early nineteenth century.

age or ability groups. The division of schools into six or seven forms is first mentioned in England in the 1520s, but may well reflect earlier practices. Such forms may literally have occupied one bench each, or more than one in a larger school like Magdalen.

The Life of the School

The official records of Magdalen College have little to say about the school between 1480 and 1540, apart from the names of the staff and occasional repairs to the building.[122] It is rare to find any mention of how it was being run, and the assumption that no news is good news should be resisted. In 1520 a chance remark during a college visitation states that the schoolmaster, Thomas Stanbridge, should be more diligent about instructing his scholars.[123] The best evidence for the social history of the school is contained in five letters in the college archives and one in the Bodleian Library. These date from between about 1496 and 1526, and illustrate some of the factors and problems in the lives of youths from their arrival at Oxford to their graduation from the university.[124] Two of the letters were written by people who were trying to get boys or youths into the college. One in about 1496 from Richard Croft, a gentleman of Chipping Norton, appeals to President Mayew on behalf of a tenant's son, who was also Croft's godson, Richard Perkyns.[125] The boy was well advanced in his learning and well disposed to learn; the president was asked to find him a place and a 'resonable eccebysion', meaning some kind of monetary support. The plea seems to have been successful, since a Perkyns occurs in 1496 as one of the choristers.[126] The other letter of about 1498 from John Etton, a college agent in Lincolnshire, begged the president for a place for his son. This was a bolder request; indeed, it was brought to Oxford by the boy himself. Etton desired his son to be given 'a sharpe creansur to se in especiall tu his lernyng and also tu his gudde rewlle', a 'creanser' (to use the normal spelling) being a tutor. He sent £2 for his son's board and a further sum of £10 for other expenses, so that the creanser might do for his son as much as he did for anyone of Etton's 'degree' or status. The father's anxiety that his boy should live according to his family's rank, and not beneath it, is palpable.[127]

[122] Some of the building references are collected in Bloxam, *Register*, III, 8, 70, 79, 90.
[123] Macray, *Register*, I, 74.
[124] The letters are printed below, pp. 75–77.
[125] For Croft's will, dated 1501, see J.R.H. Weaver and A. Beardwood (eds), *Some Oxfordshire Wills*, Oxfordshire Record Society, 39 (1958), 72–73.
[126] Below, p. 75.
[127] Below, pp. 75–76.

Etton's expectation that his son would have a creanser appears to reflect the normal practice when boys were sent to Oxford. The creanser was an adult member of the university: either a fellow of the boy's own college or another suitable adult such as a cleric. He supervised the boy's life (perhaps accommodating him in or near his own lodging) and paid his expenses, rather as (in trade) a master did with his apprentice. But he did not usually teach the boy; that was done in the grammar school. In Etton's case, the parent seems to have left the choice of creanser to the college; at other times, parents may have made their own arrangements. Naturally, the relationship between boys and their creansers could be strained by homesickness or refusal to accept discipline. A draft of a third letter, from a boy named Robert Yall to his creanser John Molesworth, fellow of Magdalen College, besought Molesworth to be a 'good master' to him and punish him 'reasonably':

> Now, yow ponys me hover much, master, and plese yow I cannot byd this ponysment. Her at fryst tyme yow dyd nott ponyse me nott hauff so much; then I dyd lerne more by yowr feyer mense then I doo now.[128]

Two more letters show the dispute between creanser and pupil at a further stage. Here the tutor has threatened to dismiss the pupil, bringing the latter in danger of leaving Oxford. An anxious communication survives from a father named Thomas Keys of Ipswich, to the president of Magdalen, apparently in the early sixteenth century. Keys had received a letter from his son Richard, a boy or youth in the college, reporting that 'his master will put hym from hym', having similarly disposed of another pupil. The parent asked the president to enquire into the situation, and pleaded for his son in the traditional manner: 'he is but yonge of age and therfor I beseke you he may have your faver, for I ham sewer he woll do muche aftur your mynde shewede to hym'.[129]

In the other case, we hear that Anthony Sutton, fellow of the college and creanser of William Shawe, 'taketh suche displeasour with him that he feareth for the same to be put out of his rome that he hath in your college at this next midsomer'. This time, the distraught father (a servant) went to Oxford himself to sort things out, bringing with him a written introduction from his employer, John Constable, a cleric of Lincoln. Constable asked the president of Magdalen that Shawe might be given a further year's residence in the college, promising that the father will 'charge him streyghtly to reforme himselff' and that, if Shawe did not in future occupy himself with virtue and learning, 'I shall never

[128] Below, p. 76.
[129] Ibid.

entreate more for him thus'.[130] Even a diligent pupil might give rise to anxiety about the rate and cost of his education, and this is the subject of the fifth letter of the group. It was written in 1513 by John Burges, a former member of the college, to President Claymond on behalf of Simon Beneson, a demy from Lincolnshire, that he might be allowed to proceed to his BA degree. Beneson had been a demy for 6 years and Burges, a family friend, asserted that the father back home 'thynkes it gretely to his rebuke that sutch as wer Symons fellos in Boston hath tornyd home maiestres of art . . . he beyng nat batchuler'. Beneson senior would not, for a hundred pounds, that 'he shuld come home withowt degree off the schole'. This letter had an effect. In the following spring, the usual time for examinations, Beneson junior did indeed determine as BA and the president received a letter of thanks from the father. Indeed, in this case the young man distinguished himself: he was promoted to a fellowship, graduated as MA, and had a career in the Church.[131]

The documentary evidence of the letters is supported by that of the Arundel and Royal *vulgaria* in their fictitious portrayal of school life. This evidence is literary and some care is needed when interpreting what it says. Sometimes the material adopts the voice of a pupil in the school:

> Gentle maister, I wolde desire iij thynges of you: onn that I myght not wake over longe of nyghtes, another that I be not bett when I com to schole; the thirde that I myghte ever emong go play me.

At other times, the speaker is the master:

> Gentle scholar, I wolde that ye shulde do iij other thynges: onn that ye ryse betymes off mornynges, another that ye go to your booke delygently, the thirde that ye behave yourselff agaynst Gode devoutely, all menn honestly, and then ye shall have youre askynge.[132]

Whose sentiments, then, are we reading in these passages: the pupils' or the master's? The likelihood is that *vulgaria* were devised and set as tasks by the master, though it is possible that some surviving examples were preserved by pupils because, to some extent, they contained the pupils' own work. In either case, *vulgaria* were part of the school curriculum and were coloured by the official culture of the school. They were primarily a means of teaching Latin, and the moral advice they contained was that of the regime. The sentiments and activities which are ascribed to the boys are likely to harmonize with those

[130] Below, p. 77.
[131] Ibid.; *BRUO* IV, 42.
[132] Nelson (ed.), *Fifteenth Century School Book*, p. 28 no. 115.

acceptable to the master, but the fact that the *vulgaria* are also sympathetic to the pupils suggests that they were reasonably close to children's experiences and outlook. We must beware, however, of assuming that we hear the pupils talking as they might have done when they were on their own.

The Arundel and Royal *vulgaria* portray a world similar to that of the letters. Boarding away from home is mentioned several times and in one case a boy's family is located in London.[133] Those who board are under the supervision of creansers, and this is recommended in order to control them and to prevent them wasting their money on dice and cards at Christmas time![134] Sometimes there is a clash between the creanser and the schoolmaster. A boy is portrayed as grieving because his creanser keeps him at home until 7.00 or 8.00 a.m. (perhaps to do menial jobs), so that he is beaten for coming late to school.[135] Days at the school began early. One passage in the *vulgaria* mentions 5.00 a.m. as the time to start, so 7.00 was quite unacceptable.[136] The days were long ones too, punctuated by a pause for breakfast and a longer break for dinner from about eleven until one, but not concluding until five or so in the afternoon. Many schools provided for the saying of prayers by the pupils every day: often for the soul of the founder, if there was one. At Wainfleet School, Waynflete laid down that every afternoon, before leaving, the scholars should say Psalm 130 (*De Profundis* — a psalm associated with praying for the dead); *Kyrie Eleyson* ('Lord have mercy upon us'); *Inclina aurem tuam* ('Lord, incline thine ear'); and *Fidelium pro animabus* (a prayer for the souls of the faithful departed).[137] We do not know if this was done at Magdalen School, but some such ritual is very likely.

The *vulgaria* do not tell us much about the structure of the day, however. Rather, they centre on its elements: learning grammar, writing and speaking Latin, and the application of the rod by the master to keep order and interest. Most *vulgaria* contain references to beating, no doubt because it was a familiar part of school life. The master who finds boys still in bed when he comes to wake them 'bryngeth a rode, stede of a candle'.[138] The boy whose creanser has

[133] Ibid., p. 16 no. 60.
[134] Ibid., p. 25 no. 104.
[135] Ibid., p. 34 no. 140. This is perhaps the problem alluded to by Waynflete in his statutes (above, p. 5).
[136] Nelson (ed.), *Fifteenth Century School Book*, p. 2 no. 1.
[137] *Statutes of the Colleges of Oxford*, Magdalen College, II, 77; Ward (ed.), *Statutes of Magdalen College*, p. 143.
[138] Nelson (ed.), *Fifteenth Century School Book*, p. 2 no. 1.

kept him late expects to be greeted with 'many a strype'.[139] Those who fail to speak Latin in school can expect to be 'sharpely punysshede', and the master is made to say that although he would like to use gentle discipline, some will never learn without beating.[140] Even the boys may have been enlisted in helping with this: we sometimes hear in schools that they had to pull down the breeches of the culprit brought up to be punished. In one of the Arundel passages, a schoolboy remarks that

> It is a noble sporte for me to here the fasynge [i.e. bravado] and brallynge [i.e. blustering] of thies boys when they shall be accusede off custos, and to se how subtyll every man is in defendyng himself.[141]

Nelson explains 'custos' as a 'senior pupil, monitor', but this does not do justice to the office. In sixteenth-century practice, to which this Magdalen passage is one of the earliest witnesses, a 'custos' was a boy who had produced bad work or given wrong answers. When the class was being taught, he was the first to be made to repeat the lesson or reply to questions. He sometimes had a stick to use on the other boys if they were idle or spoke English in class, and he could question them, with the proviso that anyone giving an incorrect reply became custos in his turn.[142] This was meant to keep the boys lively and stop them becoming idle as a group, but one can well imagine the bickering to which it gave rise. The Magdalen reference leaves it open as to how many 'custodes' existed but it is likely that there were more than one, just as it is that the school was divided into forms.

At first sight, the recurrence of remarks about beating suggests a culture of regular corporal punishment. This may well have been true, but the frequency of such references suggests that matters were less straightforward. It appears that beating did not happen as often as its supporters would have liked. A passage in the *vulgaria* declares that 'some think themselves too old and too great to be beat with the rod . . . Howbeit, when I came first to this university, there was no difference in correction between great and small'. It concludes, 'good rule goeth backward'.[143] Parents were blamed for indulging their children and opposing corporal punishment:

[139] Ibid., p. 34 no. 140.
[140] Ibid., pp. 34–35 nos 143–44.
[141] Ibid., p. 41 no. 176.
[142] H.C. Maxwell-Lyte, *A History of Eton College (1440–1910)*, 4th edn (London, 1911), 139–40; White (ed.), *Vulgaria*, p. liv.
[143] Nelson (ed.), *Fifteenth Century School Book*, p. 31 no. 126.

I will make you an example [says a character in the *vulgaria*], by a cousin of mine that [was sent] to his ABC [school] at the next door, and if he come weeping after his master hath chared away the fleas from his skin, anon his mother looketh on his buttocks if the stripes be seen. And the stripes appear, she weepeth and waileth and fareth as she were mad; then she complaineth of the cruelty of teachers, saying she had rather see her child were fair buried than so to be entreated.

The result of this attitude, observes the author, is that when children grow up, 'they wax bold to do all mischievousness . . . and at the last, after their merits, some be hanged, some be headed . . . and when they come to that end they curse the fathers and mothers and others that had rule of them in their youth'.[144] Equally, the boys had methods of avoiding punishment. The schoolmaster complains that

As sone as I am cum into the scole, this felow goith to make water, and he goyth oute to the comyn drafte. Sone after, another askith licence that he may go drynke; another callith upon me that he may have licence to go home. Thies and such other leyth my scholars for excuse oftyntyms that they may be oute of the waye.[145]

Clearly not everyone tolerated beating, either parents or pupils, and Robert Yall's protest is echoed in the *vulgaria*.

Schools like Magdalen had various problems to contend with, as schools have now. The *vulgaria* worry about discipline and motivation. They articulate the common feeling of that age (and one still heard today) that problems begin at home with parental indulgence. A famous passage in the Arundel *vulgaria* describes, from the mouth of a pupil, how delightfully he lived at home until he was ten: having his breakfast in bed, getting up only when persuaded to do so, and putting on clothes laid ready for him. Now, he complains, he has to follow the strict hours of school, rise early, study his book, and endure the rod.[146] The unstated message of the passage is that discipline is needed to counteract the indulgence of home life. Another problem was the range of abilities in the classroom. The talented sat side by side with the wealthy or well-patronized who had gained entry to the school without the ability to profit from it:

Sum scholars there be [observes the writer], but ther ar very few of them, that have goode wyttes and kepe styll in remembrance that as they here; and sum have a goode perceyvynge with them. . . but they forgete more in a day than they lurnede in iij; sum ther ar that be so dull which withoute great laboure cannot cane [i.e. know] the leste thynge.[147]

144 Ibid., pp. 13–14 no. 52.
145 Ibid., p. 39 no. 165.
146 Ibid., pp. 2–3 no. 1.
147 Ibid., p. 35 no. 145.

There might be bullying:

I can not be in rest her for your Antony, wich dyd bete me abowt the hede and abowt the face yesterda with his fistes, so that for ache this nyght y cauld be no maner a menys fayl aslepe.[148]

And violence beyond the school gates:

Ther ys a scolar in owr hall that had a lytyll besines to doe in the towne the laste weke. He went owt to do hit in the evenyng unhappaly, with whome thre goynge lyke scolares (but the were thevys in very deyde) meyt hym abowght viijt of the cloke as he was comyng hom agayne. One of them steppyd to hym and stoppyd his moyth with one of his handes, leset he shold crye owt, and with the tother hand he pomelyd hym abowth the payte to make him amasyd. The meyne whyll the secunde pluckyd away his pures and all the mone that was in hit. The iijrde stode a good way of, wachyng lest any shold cum apon them sodenly.[149]

Five centuries later education has not eradicated these problems; they are still with us.

What we do not have to the same extent as early Tudor schools are epidemics: the often fatal outbreaks of plague and the sweat. At Winchester College, thirty-four of the scholars admitted between 1395 and 1410 (out of a total entry of 406) died while attending the school, about eight per cent.[150] Masters themselves were not immune from death. Anwykyll died in office at an unknown age; Scarbot at about 32; Holt at about 34. Even Stanbridge was dead before he was 50. The Arundel *vulgaria*, written in the 1490s, contain three passages about the pestilence: one about being sick of it and two about those it has killed.[151] The Royal, apparently dating from a decade or two later, have five.[152] When a country soothsayer claims to foretell the weather, someone wishes him to be asked if he thought it 'a yere of helth or of syknes'.[153] At school, two scholars fall ill with stomach pains, one of them believing that he has perhaps eaten a bad herring. At once there is an alarm and boys are withdrawn from the school; when the scholars recover, a message is sent out to bring the others back, since all is well.[154] To cope with epidemics, college communities moved from Oxford to one or more of their manors in the countryside. This is first recorded at Magdalen in 1485 and took place every few years after that, especially after

[148] Orme, *Education and Society*, p. 139 no. 32.
[149] Ibid., p. 145 no. 66.
[150] Kirby, *Winchester Scholars*, pp. 22–38.
[151] Nelson (ed.), *Fifteenth Century School Book*, p. 45 no. 196, p. 83 no. 349, p. 87 no. 364.
[152] Orme, *Education and Society*, p. 137 nos 22–23, p. 140 no. 36, p. 143 no. 55, p. 147 no. 78.
[153] Ibid., p. 140 no. 36.
[154] Ibid., p. 137 nos 22–23.

1500. The fellows and scholars of Magdalen went, on different occasions, to Brackley (Northants.), Brailes (War.), Ewelme (Oxon.), Wallingford (Berks.), and Witney (Oxon.).[155] There they lodged where they could, often only in farms and cottages.

The school went with them, a fact that enters into the *vulgaria*. 'When we last [went] forthe from the universite for sikenes, we had a fole slutty kechyn for owr scole, but now we be provydyd of a place a lityl more honest, how be it is but a stable.'[156] Such a migration provided a welcome break from routine and new experiences, but not everyone in the classroom necessarily moved with the school. The non-collegiate boys would have had difficulty in doing so, and in their case the school was as good as closed:

> I was from scole a grett part of this last yere' [complains a speaker], and that be the reason of sykenes that contynyd her in the towne. God gyve grace that it begyne not agen this here, for and if it do, I shall shortly go hense, for my fryndes have determynd to send me awa to another place wher the thinke I ma go to scole withe less juperty [i.e. jeopardy].[157]

There is, in fact, a record of boys being taken elsewhere in this way. In 1503, the registers of Winchester College note the entry of six boys from Oxford, after 25 years in which only three had been admitted at all.[158] This surge is likely to reflect the outbreaks of plague in Oxford in 1501 and 1503, and the resolve of some parents to send their boys away to school. It is worth remembering that the threat of disease was a potent force in educational history, no less than new theories and curricula. It ruled what parents did and scholars learnt, irrespective of the change from late medieval culture to that of humanism.

155 Wood, *Colleges and Halls*, vol. I, col. 651; Macray, *Register*, I, 16–33, passim.
156 Orme, *Education and Society*, p. 147 no. 78.
157 Ibid., p. 143 no. 55.
158 Kirby, *Winchester Scholars*, p. 99.

4. THE SCHOOL AND ENGLISH EDUCATION, 1480–1540

The Magdalen Diaspora

Waynflete founded his school when the teaching of grammar in Oxford had fallen into decline. In the long term, his initiative provided a valuable amenity for the university and the city. Briefly, it even restored the place of Oxford as a leading centre of school teaching. Anwykyll was a pioneer; Stanbridge and Holt found ready employment elsewhere. But by 1500 Oxford's importance as a major centre of grammar was again ebbing away. There was more than one reason for this. In the first place, the school did not stimulate other important schools to open up in Oxford. Indeed, in 1492 the university officers who had supervised the grammar schools in the past were said to have no duties left to perform.[159] Lack of opportunity to teach in Oxford meant that masters and pupils of Magdalen School who sought such work had to find it in other towns. They took their skills elsewhere and thereby eroded Oxford's originality as a centre of humanist grammar. The development of printing was another factor. Briefly, from about 1478 into the early 1480s, there were printers in Oxford, one of whom published the work of Anwykyll. Subsequently, however, the printing of schoolbooks was largely based in London, and Oxford's needs in this respect were supplied from the capital, not vice versa.

There are other signs that, after 1500, Magdalen School was not regarded as the only standard of good and modern teaching, or even as the chief one. Some early sixteenth-century school statutes specify that the teaching of grammar should follow a particular model, and if this evidence is collected the result is illuminating (table 1). Magdalen was the model in only one of these cases; in the rest, the standard was taken from schools or masters elsewhere. In 1521, three leading grammarians (Horman, Lily, and Whittington) discussed teaching methods in print, with personal attacks, in the so-called Grammarians' War. Although Lily was an ex-pupil of Magdalen School, none of the three by 1521 was based in Oxford and their writings were published in London.[160]

[159] *Statuta Antiqua*, ed. by Gibson, p. 300.

[160] On the grammarians' war, see White (ed.), *Vulgaria*, pp. xxiii–xxxii. The masters concerned were Lily and Whittington, based in London, and Horman, based at Eton (ibid.).

Table 1. *School Statutes in the Early Sixteenth Century*

Date	School	County	School or Grammar Chosen as Model
1511	Wimborne	Dorset	Eton and Winchester[161]
1520	Bruton	Som.	Magdalen College or St Paul's[162]
1525	Manchester	Lancs.	Banbury, alias Stanbridge, grammar[163]
1525	Saffron Walden	Essex	Eton or Winchester[164]
1526	Warrington	Lancs.	Whittington's grammar[165]
1528	Cuckfield	Sussex	Eton[166]

Still, Magdalen College and its school were to have an important influence on school education after the 1480s in less formal ways. Magdalen schoolmasters and pupils went to teach elsewhere and a few (usually after leaving Oxford) published school textbooks (Fig. 15). The first known journey away from Magdalen to another school was that of Stanbridge, but his travels in the 1490s are still imperfectly known. As we have seen, they may have taken him to teach at Winchcombe and Lichfield before he reached Banbury. More certain is the career of John Holt who took the experience of teaching in Magdalen School to Lambeth Palace, Chichester School, and the household of Prince Henry.[167] The first and last of Holt's appointments were clearly influential ones, but Chichester School was significant too. Although this school is not famous in educational history, it had a good standing in the early Tudor period. Edward Storey, the local bishop, refounded it in 1499, making the tuition free and endowing the master with a salary derived from the cathedral prebend of Highleigh — hence the school's later name of the Prebendal School. The prebend also conferred status; it admitted an English schoolmaster to the Church aristocracy of cathedral clergy for the first time since the twelfth century.[168] Headmasters even of Winchester and Eton left to teach at Chichester in the 1520s and 1530s. Holt was not the first master of the reordered school, but he was the first with a humanist background, and one of his successors was another Magdalen man, John Goldyve.

[161] Orme, *Education in the West of England*, p. 185.
[162] Ibid., p. 121.
[163] *VCH Lancashire*, II, ed. by W. Farrer and J. Brownbill (London, 1908), 583.
[164] *VCH Essex*, II, ed. by W. Page and J.H. Round (London, 1907), 521.
[165] *VCH Lancashire*, II, 601.
[166] *VCH Sussex*, II, ed. by W. Page (London, 1907), 416–17.
[167] Orme, 'John Holt', pp. 286–90.
[168] On the history of the school, see A.F. Leach, 'Schools', in *VCH Sussex* , II, 402–03. The masters after 1497 are listed in John Le Neve, *Fasti Ecclesiae Anglicanae 1300–1541*, VII: *Chichester Diocese*, ed. by Joyce M. Horn (London, 1964), 30.

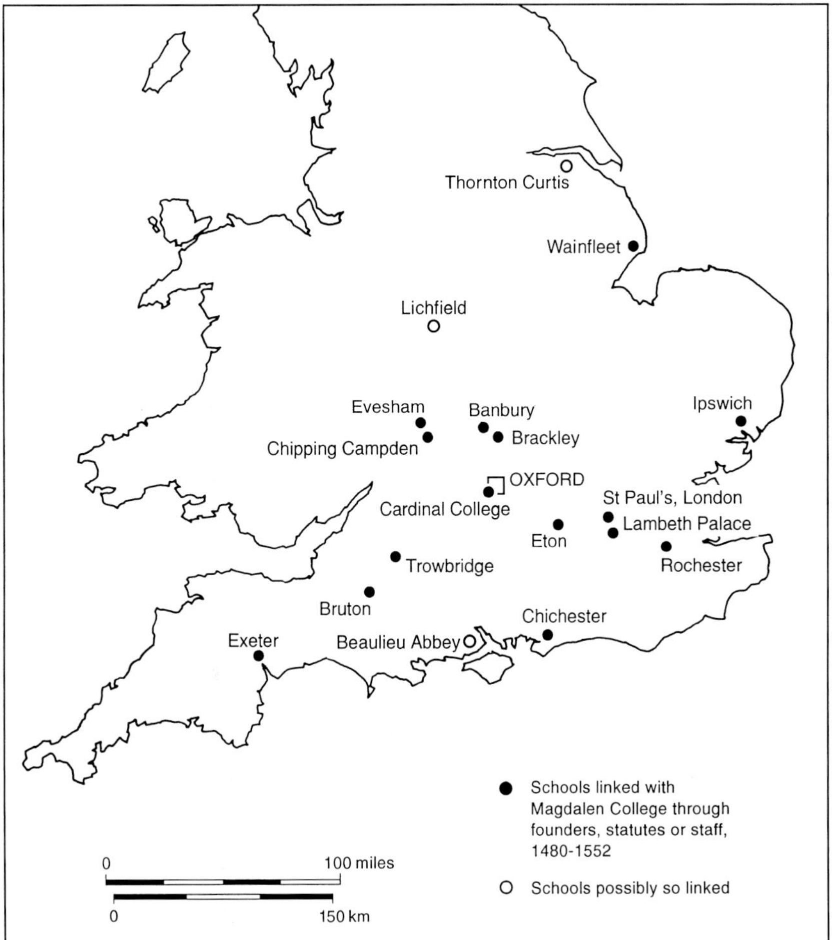

FIG. 15. Links between Magdalen College, its school, and schools elsewhere in England.

The next important school to be colonized from Magdalen was Banbury. This was a new foundation, endowed by the bishop of Lincoln, William Smith, who was also the co-founder of Brasenose College Oxford.[169] In 1501 Smith appointed John Stanbridge master of the hospital of St John outside the south gate of Banbury, an institution which, like many contemporary hospitals, seems

[169] The history of the school is briefly dealt with in *VCH Oxfordshire*, I, 461–62 and II, 152–54.

to have lost most of its original functions. Stanbridge and his successors bore the title 'master of the hospital', but their function was chiefly to teach a grammar school. Smith, like Storey, wished to improve the standing of his schoolmaster. The master's salary (about £10) was not unusually high,[170] but Smith allowed Stanbridge to combine the post with a parish benefice and even added a third promotion: one of the less valuable prebends of Lincoln Cathedral.[171] The connection of Banbury School with Magdalen College became a close one. Stanbridge remained there until his death in 1510, and although Smith then appointed a Brasenose man, John Crag, Crag did not last for more than a few months and may have been a temporary appointment.[172] The permanent replacement for Stanbridge was Thomas Brinknell who had already been master of Magdalen School and who ruled at Banbury from 1511 until his death in 1539. Brinknell was a doctor of divinity, an unusually high distinction for a schoolmaster, and Smith secured him by granting him a prebend of Lincoln Cathedral worth £12 on the day he appointed him to the hospital.[173] In 1517, Magdalen College School received Thomas Stanbridge, a former usher of Banbury and probably a relation of John, as its master,[174] and when Brinknell died his successor was appointed from Magdalen College. This was Nicholas Cartwright, another DD, and while the bishop of Lincoln (now John Longland) did not give him a canonry, Cartwright was able to hold a parish benefice along with the school and even gained permission to hold a third promotion.[175] As he ruled until the hospital was dissolved in 1548, Banbury had an almost uninterrupted series of masters from Magdalen during the first half of the sixteenth century. Indeed, it was virtually a second Magdalen School, able to attract scholars from the centre of England while lying at a respectful distance from Oxford.

Teachers from Magdalen soon dispersed to other places. William Andrew, usher in the college school in about 1497, appears in 1505 as master of Exeter High School, one of the larger provincial cathedral schools. A second Magdalen

[170] Ibid., II, 153; *Valor Ecclesiasticus tempore Henrici VIII auctoritate regis institutus*, ed. by J. Caley, 6 vols (London, 1810–24), II, 164.
[171] *BRUO* III, 1754–55.
[172] *VCH Oxfordshire*, II, 153–54; *BRUO* IV, 148.
[173] *BRUO* I, 268. The prebend, Marston St Lawrence, was worth £12 5*s*. in 1535 (*Valor Ecclesiasticus*, IV, 21).
[174] *BRUO* IV, 533. As Thomas was much younger than John, it is unlikely that they were brothers and the relationship was probably that of uncle and nephew, or cousins.
[175] *BRUO* IV, 106.

usher, Philip Fryer, followed him there in 1521.[176] In 1507, Eton College appointed a headmaster from Magdalen, John Goldyve, who had been usher in 1499–1500 and later left Eton for Chichester.[177] Then it was the turn of St Paul's School London. This ancient cathedral school was itself re-endowed as a free school by John Colet, dean of St Paul's, between 1508 and 1512. Colet was even more ambitious than Smith and Storey to raise the status of schoolmasters and the standard of recruits. He gave the high master, or headmaster, of St Paul's the huge salary of £34 — more than three times that of the standard £10 thought sufficient in most endowed schools; even the surmaster (second master) got £17. Colet's first high master was another of the early Magdalen humanist grammarians. William Lily had been a demy of the college in the early 1480s and therefore, presumably, a pupil in the school under Anwykyll. He left the college, travelled in the Mediterranean, followed further classical studies, and married. In 1509, Colet appointed him to St Paul's, and by 1515 Lily had a Magdalen colleague as surmaster, Maurice Birchynshaw. There seems to have been a connection between St Paul's, Magdalen, and Banbury in the 1510s. In the 1519 edition of the *Vulgaria* ascribed to John Stanbridge, the *vulgaria* themselves are said to be 'compiled, together with their vernacular equivalents, according to the custom of the school of St Paul's'.[178] When Richard FitzJames, bishop of London, endowed a school at Bruton (Somerset) in 1520, he laid down that it should teach grammar 'after the good new form used in Magdalen College in Oxford, or in the school of Paul's in London', implying that their teaching would be similar.[179]

Men trained at Magdalen are known to have gone to teach at other schools up to the mid-sixteenth century, including Brackley (Northants.), Chipping Campden (Glos.), Evesham (Worcs.), Cardinal College (Oxford), Rochester (Kent), and Trowbridge (Wilts.).[180] Beaulieu Abbey (Hants.) and Thornton College (Lincs.) are other possible places.[181] Wainfleet too might be expected to have received its staff from Magdalen since the college president made the appointments, but members of the college appear to have regarded that place with little favour. We know the names of eight masters of Wainfleet School from 1466 to 1555,[182] and only one of them has yet been identified as probably

[176] Orme, *Education in the West of England*, pp. 56–57.
[177] *BRUO* II, 788.
[178] White (ed.), *Vulgaria*, p. 13.
[179] Orme, *Education in the West of England*, p. 121.
[180] Below, pp. 73–4.
[181] Ibid.
[182] Below, p. 72.

educated at Magdalen. This is William Dobyll (master *c*.1493–95), who may be identical with a Dobyll (Christian name unknown) recorded as a chorister and demy of Magdalen in 1485–93.[183] Thomas Brinknell, who succeeded Dobyll in 1495, became a member of Magdalen in later years, but he was an alumnus of Lincoln College (Oxford) when he went to Wainfleet.[184] No doubt the remoteness of Wainfleet made it unattractive to anyone who did not have connections with the area. One school absolutely refused to employ grammarians from Magdalen: Winchester College. As we have already noticed, it ceased to appoint outsiders after the middle of the fifteenth century, and confined its masters solely to its own alumni and those of its sister foundation, New College Oxford.

The evidence for this diaspora may grow in future, as more schoolmasters are identified and their biographies researched. At the same time, it would be wrong to imply that humanist grammar was diffused only from Magdalen, even in the 1480s. There were other early humanist teachers, including Wykehamist ones. John Stanbridge came to Magdalen from New College, and William Horman, who was at the same college while Anwykyll and Stanbridge were teaching in Magdalen, became a leading humanist schoolmaster first at Winchester and later at Eton. The records of Wykehamists' careers in the early Tudor period show that a number of them taught in grammar schools in the south of England — as many as have yet been connected with Magdalen. Smaller lists of schoolmasters can be linked with All Souls and Merton at Oxford and St John's in Cambridge. Moreover, once humanist grammar was well diffused, Magdalen became less special for teaching it. The candle first to be lit looks duller when the room is full of lights. Between about 1483 and the late 1490s, the College School was well ahead of most of the field nationally. After that, it was still an important school for Oxford, but it no longer had the distinction of its first few years.

Magdalen and School Textbooks

The other way in which humanist grammar was diffused to the rest of England was through textbooks. Anwykyll not only taught grammar — he published it. His patron William Waynflete seems to have appreciated the possibility of spreading humanist Latin through a written textbook, mass-produced in print. Table 2 lists the grammar writers and the editions of their textbooks printed in

[183] Bloxam, *Register*, I, I; IV, 25.
[184] *BRUO* I, 268.

Table 2. *English Grammars printed in England or for England 1480–1530*

Author	No. of editions	Place of education	Base when writing
Anonymous	39	—	—
Anwykyll, John	8	Cambridge	Oxford
Barkby, John	1	London?	London
Colet, John and Wm Lily	6	Oxford	London
Holt, John	6	Oxford	London
Horman, William	4	Oxford	Winchester/Eton
Mancinelli, Antonio	2	Italy	Italy
Perotti, Niccolo	2	Italy	Italy
Stanbridge, John	107	Oxford	Banbury
Sulpizio, Giovanni	8	Italy	Italy
Whittington, Robert	181	Lichfield?/Oxford	In or near London

England or for the English market during this period. These figures underestimate grammarians from continental Europe whose works could be imported in editions printed outside England. But they show that among the English writers of schoolbooks, people with Oxford connections were dominant and that, within the Oxford group, grammarians linked with Magdalen were important. Stanbridge is the outstanding name with Magdalen affiliations, and he was surpassed in the number of editions of his schoolbooks before 1530 by only one other writer. This was Robert Whittington, that prolific author and combative man whom Oxford historians have traditionally regarded as another member of Magdalen College and a disciple of Stanbridge there. The theory was apparently formulated by Anthony Wood, who wished to establish the Oxford credentials of as many scholars as he could, and has been repeated by Bloxam and Emden.[185] However, there is no contemporary evidence that Whittington studied at Magdalen College or School. Indeed, he is not recorded as having any Oxford connection until 1513, when he was laureated as a poet and given the degree of BA on the grounds that he had been a schoolmaster for twelve years and studied rhetoric for fourteen.[186] He called himself 'Lichfeldensis' (that is, of Lichfield) and, as has been suggested above, his connection with Stanbridge

[185] Wood, *Athenae Oxonienses*, vol. I, col. 55; Bloxam, *Register*, III, 11; *BRUO* III, 2039, currently the best account of Whittington's career but capable of amplification.

[186] OUA, Register of Congregation, G, fols 172ᵛ, 173ᵛ, 187; *BRUO* III, 2039.

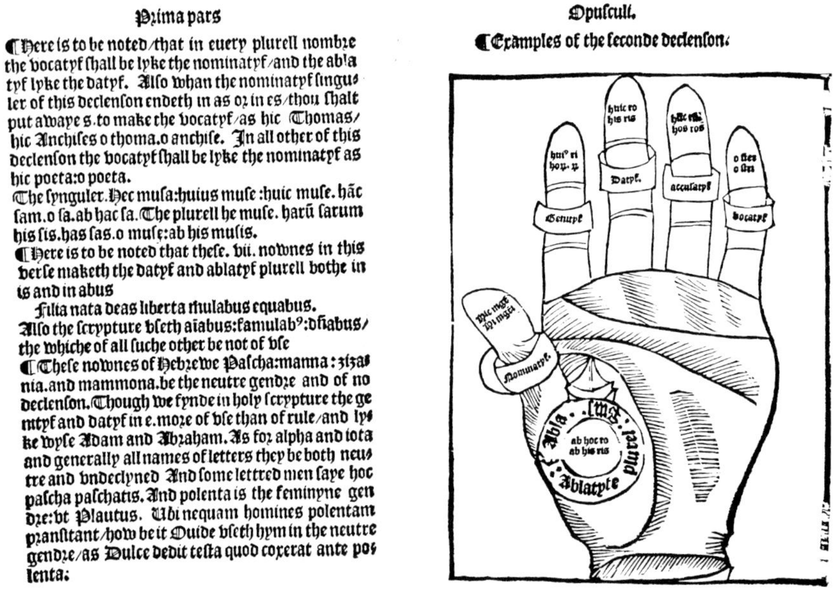
Prima pars

Here is to be noted/that in every plurell nombre the vocatyf shall be lyke the nominatyf/and the ablatyf lyke the datyf. Also whan the nominatyf singuler of this declenson endeth in as or in es/thou shalt put awaye s.to make the vocatyf/as hic Thomas/hic Anchises o thoma.o anchise. In all other of this declenson the vocatyf shall be lyke the nominatyf as hic poeta:o poeta.

The synguler. Hec musa:huius muse :huic muse. hãc sam.o sa.ab hac sa. The plurell he muse. harũ sarum his sis.has sas.o muse:ab his musis.

Here is to be noted that these. vii. nownes in this verse maketh the datyf and ablatyf plurell bothe in is and in abus

Filia nata deas liberta mulabus equabus.

Also the scrypture vseth aĩabus:famulab⁹:dñabus/the whiche of all suche other be not of vse

These nownes of Hebrewe Pascha:manna:zizania.and mammona.be the neutre gendre and of no declenson. Though we fynde in holy scrypture the genityf and datyf in e.more of vse than of rule/and lyke wyse Adam and Abraham. As for alpha and iota and generally all names of letters they be both neutre and vndeclyned And some lettred men saye hoc pascha paschatis. And polenta is the feminyne gendre:vt Plautus. Ubi nequam homines polentam pransitant/how be it Ouide vseth hym in the neutre gendre/as Dulce dedit testa quod coxerat ante polenta:

Opuscull.

Examples of the seconde declenson.

FIG. 16. An illustration from John Holt's *Lac Puerorum*, showing a rare use of a diagram to help pupils remember the cases of Latin nouns and the paradigms of *hic magister*, 'the schoolmaster'.

is more likely to have been forged there or nearby than in Oxford.[187] He was a beneficiary of the Magdalen diaspora, but it has yet to be proved that he was linked with Magdalen directly.

Let us now look at the writings of the Magdalen grammarians in more detail. Anwykyll's works were printed at Oxford in 1483, at London in the same year, at Antwerp in 1486, and at Deventer in 1489.[188] These Netherlands editions were probably intended for the English market rather than for use in continental schools. His textbooks stayed in print until 1529, forty years after his death, no bad achievement even by modern standards, but he was alone in publishing a schoolbook while working at Magdalen School. The next Magdalen writer of a grammar, John Holt, had left the college and was teaching at Lambeth Palace when his work appeared. Its title was *Lac Puerorum, or Mylke for Children*, and it was probably first printed between 1496 and 1498.[189] Holt's book is a

[187] Above, p. 18.
[188] STC 695–696.7 (*Compendium*); 23904–08 (*Vulgaria*).
[189] On what follows, see Orme, 'John Holt', pp. 291–303.

basic grammar teaching the eight parts of speech, declensions of nouns, conjugations of verbs, basic syntax, and so on. Its distinctive feature is its three pictorial woodcuts. Fifteenth- and sixteenth-century grammars, whether in manuscript or print, are not set out with much visual emphasis: they are simply in prose without tables, let alone pictures. The first woodcut depicts a hand to show the case endings of the second declension of nouns (Fig. 16), and the second another hand with the endings of the pronoun *hic*, *haec*, *hoc*. For his third picture, Holt wanted to display the case endings of all five declensions of nouns, but a hand was not big enough for this purpose so he supplied an engraving of six candles. Hands were already used in books as the basis of diagrams and they occur in at least one continental schoolbook of this period. Holt therefore did not invent the device but he was the first to use it in an English grammar. His book survives in at least five editions issued between 1505 and 1511, but it was not reprinted afterwards and no other writer adopted his policy of illustration. Perhaps pictures were thought by other grammarians to stoop too much to conquer, to pander too much to the young.

The most influential of the Magdalen, or rather ex-Magdalen, grammarians was undoubtedly John Stanbridge at Banbury School from 1501 to 1510. In about 1505, the London printer William Pynson printed a book called the *Accidence*, a basic Latin grammar in English, which he described as 'Maister Stanbridges awne makyng'.[190] This was reproduced by Pynson and other printers in dozens of editions during the next thirty years. Other basic school texts in English appeared after 1505 with Stanbridge's name on their title-pages. They include *Parvula* (*c.*1507) which explains how to do Latin composition, *Gradus Comparationum* (*c.*1509) on the comparison of adjectives, *Sum es fui* on the forms of *esse* and some other common irregular verbs (*c.*1510), a basic *Vocabula* or Latin–English vocabulary in verse (1510), and a collection of *Vulgaria* (*c.*1509).[191] By 1510, the year Stanbridge died, his name was attached to a set of basic schoolbooks which taught the whole elementary part of the grammar course. No such set by a single author or editor had previously been available in print, since early schoolbooks like Anwykyll's and Holt's were usually individual works that had to be used in tandem with others. Stanbridge was teaching and writing at a time when printers in England had at last begun to master their trade and their markets. Printing, for all its technological

[190] STC 23139.5.

[191] On these works, see STC II, 359–63, esp. nos. 23139.5, 23155.9, 23156, 231642, 23178, and 23195.5.

importance, had been slower to develop in England than on the continent. It was more effective at first in producing quality goods than in cheap mass production. By 1510, the public was more used to printed books and the printers had more capital and expertise to make, distribute, and sell them. Stanbridge thus became the first large-selling school textbook author, and his books remained immensely popular for the next thirty years, coming out in numerous editions from various printing houses. Like some other great pioneers, he was dead when this happened.

The question of the authorship of the works ascribed to Stanbridge is a delicate one. The *Accidence* of about 1505 is the only one to be described as 'of Maister Stanbridges awne makynge'. *Sum es fui* and the *Vocabula* are simply 'of Stanbridge' and the title of *Vulgaria Stanbrige* effectively says the same thing. The title-pages of *Gradus Comparationum* and *Parvula* are more circumspect and claim merely to be *ex Stanbrigiana editione*, 'from the Stanbridgian edition'.[192] This caution was appropriate because most of Stanbridge's schoolbooks were not such original creations as bibliographers and historians used to suppose. Rather, their format follows the works of John Leland written at Oxford in the early fifteenth century. Leland anticipated Stanbridge in providing a complete range of elementary textbooks in English, teaching Latin grammar and syntax. His works circulated widely in manuscript during the fifteenth century, and individual schoolmasters altered and revised them in small ways. When printers in England and the Netherlands began to exploit the English market for schoolbooks, they seized on the Leland textbooks and printed them. This started in 1482 when the Oxford printer Theodoric Rood brought out the *Parvula*, the basic book in the Leland tradition on how to compose Latin, and by 1500 there were several different versions of these texts in print. The originality of Stanbridge, it seems, was to edit them. He corrected usage and style to accord with classical Latin; sometimes he inserted quotations from classical authors to demonstrate particular points. This strategy was successful. Schoolmasters were given texts of the kind they knew — texts that followed traditional layout, order of teaching, and even phraseology, while supplying the new, sought-after humanist models and standards.

Early printed grammars like those of Anwykyll, Stanbridge, and Whittington appear difficult to use today because they lack a visual dimension — even a tabular approach. This did not worry contemporaries, and Holt's use of pictures did not inspire others to follow him. But printers used one device to

[192] For references, see the previous note.

make their grammars attractive. They put in a decorated title-page, showing a school at work. This idea was not an English invention. Pictures of schools had appeared in manuscripts, and the practice was introduced into schoolbooks in the Netherlands and Germany in the late fifteenth century.[193] The idea was adopted in turn by printers based in England; the first such picture was issued in London in 1495 by Wynkyn de Worde, who used or copied a woodcut of Netherlands origin.[194] Pictorial title-pages were meant to make the book look attractive, and one suspects that printers wished to use such pictures to make their school books appeal to schoolmasters. It may well have been the masters who bought most copies in the first instance, and then sold them on to their pupils. Certainly, de Worde's picture portrays a master in a school as every master would like to have been portrayed (Fig. 17). He sits enthroned in a huge chair, the embodiment of magisterial authority. He holds his birch, the attribute of his office. The school, in as far as it is shown, is well ordered. Three representative pupils, earnestly attentive, sit at the master's feet with such self-discipline that the birch does not need to be used. It rests in the master's left hand.

In 1496 Richard Pynson, de Worde's chief English rival in producing schoolbooks, produced a schoolroom scene of his own, or rather borrowed it from a continental source.[195] His picture shows a master at a desk with obedient pupils, but in a much more magnificent environment (Fig. 18). The schoolroom looks as large as the Divinity School in Oxford and the master's seat is backed by a cloth of estate like that of a royal throne. It appears that this picture was not a success, for it was withdrawn within about a year. Perhaps it lent itself to ridicule; very likely the schoolmaster, dressed continental fashion in a high hat and wielding a cane not a birch, caused amusement in England. At any rate, in 1497 Pynson commissioned a new and original woodcut of a school closer to English usage (Fig. 19). The schoolroom is now less grand, although it possesses a well-tiled floor. The master has a hat in the English style; he holds a proper English birch; and, to encourage trade, the pupils are shown with books. In the properly organized English school — ran the message — all pupils will have their own printed copies. So successful was this cut that not only did Pynson

[193] On this subject, see William Martin Conway, *The Woodcutters of the Netherlands in the Fifteenth Century* (Cambridge, 1884), esp. pp. 228–29, 294.

[194] Edward Hodnett, *English Woodcuts 1480–1535*, 2nd edn. (Oxford, 1973), pp. 11, 263 no. 918 (fig. 75).

[195] Ibid., p. 348 no. 1507a (fig. 139).

FIG. 17 (top left). Schoolmaster and pupils, from a Netherlands woodcut reused by Wynkyn de Worde in schoolbooks of the 1490s.

FIG. 18 (top right). Schoolmaster and pupils, from a Netherlands woodcut reused by Richard Pynson for his 1496 edition of the Hymnal.

FIG. 19 (left). Schoolmaster and pupils, from the new woodcut used by Richard Pynson for his 1497 edition of the Hymnal.

display it in his schoolbooks, but Wynkyn de Worde produced a version of his own and used it repeatedly.[196]

Apart from these illustrated title-pages, there was no great difference between manuscript and printed schoolbooks or pre-humanist and humanist ones. Nevertheless, the technology of printing brought about changes in the schoolroom as time went on. First of all, printing created problems. The basic schoolbooks like the *Accidence* and the *Parvula* were popular and widely used, but there was no standard text. On the contrary, several versions circulated: pre-humanist and humanist, longer and shorter, Wynkyn de Worde editions, Richard Pynson editions, and Dutch editions. The compositors who set the type introduced further variations: a Dutchman was not necessarily the best person to produce a consistent English text![197] A schoolmaster, going to a stationer's to buy more copies, might find that his usual edition was no longer available and that a different one was in stock. Pupils might turn up with further dissimilar versions. This variety had existed in the manuscript period as well, but then individual schoolbooks had mattered less. There were now more books about, yet uniformity was still elusive. In 1526 Leonard Cox, an English schoolmaster then working in Poland, advised teachers to read each text aloud to their pupils, enabling them 'to correct whatever mistakes they notice in their own copies, to fill in gaps and rub out what does not appear in the teacher's text'.[198] If this were done, it must have been a laborious procedure. There were also variations between the grammatical authors used in different schools. Eton, as we have seen, employed Stanbridge and Lily while Winchester College preferred Stanbridge and Sulpizio. It is not surprising to find a decree of the English Church, issued at London in 1530, claiming that a boy who moved from one school to another through plague or the master's death would encounter such different methods that he would be 'almost laughed at by all, and so it happens that those who are still raw in grammar suffer great loss in the progress of their learning'.[199]

[196] Ibid., pp. 12, 34–35, 266 no. 922 (fig. 80), p. 348 no. 1508 (fig. 140).

[197] The variations in text are well illustrated by Hedwig Gwosdek (ed.), *Early Printed Editions of the Long Accidence and Short Accidence Grammars* (Heidelberg, 1991), passim.

[198] L. Cox, *De Erudienda Iuventute* (Cracow, 1526), section 17, printed in A. Breeze and J. Glomski, 'An Early Treatise upon Education: Leonard Cox's *De Erudienda Iuventute* (1526)', *Humanistica Lovaniensia*, 40 (1991), 112–67 at 142–43.

[199] D. Wilkins (ed.), *Concilia Magnae Britanniae et Hiberniae, 446–1717*, 4 vols (London, 1737), III, 722–23, trans. in A.F. Leach, *Educational Charters and Documents, 598–1909* (Cambridge, 1911), pp. 446–47.

Printing, as well as causing these problems, could solve them. It was possible in principle to have uniform texts. Printers had the capability, if such texts could be agreed on, to reproduce them in sufficient numbers for the whole country. But that was not a decision the printers could reach by themselves. They were competing with short-term objectives, and some authority was needed to bring them to order. Here Wolsey came in. It looks as though, in the 1520s, he made the first attempt to standardize school textbooks. As an ex-schoolmaster, currently trying to found a big Eton-style boarding school at Ipswich, he would have been aware of the problems of diversity. As the leading figure in the English Church, he would have understood the need to control religious books, now that Luther and others were writing. In 1529 the London printer Peter Treveris published the grammar approved by Wolsey for Ipswich school. The title reads, in translation, 'The rudiments of grammar and the method of teaching, not merely of the school of Ipswich happily established by the most reverend Lord Thomas, Cardinal of York, but also prescribed for all the other schools in the whole of England'.[200] Treveris was anticipating such a decision rather than following one, because no order to this effect is known, but it looks as though Wolsey was intending to make his approved grammar compulsory nationally. In the end, perhaps, he was persuaded that more consultation was needed. In 1530, the English Church agreed to set up a committee to decide on an authorized grammar,[201] but other things intervened: Henry VIII's divorce and the break with Rome. When Henry became head of the Church in 1534, the initiative in the matter passed to him, but Henry was more interested in property than prepositions during the 1530s. It was not until 1540 that he found time to impose an authorized grammar. The grammar chosen for this purpose was based on that of St Paul's, edited by John Colet its founder and William Lily its first master. For the rest of the sixteenth century, most English schools used it and uniformity was, at last, achieved.[202]

Education and Society, 1480–1540

The issue of uniformity leads us into the history of early Tudor England. What effects had government, religion, and society upon schools, and what effects had schools on them in return? The first of these questions is the easier to answer. Magdalen School was a product of its time: its endowed, collegiate framework and free education were characteristic of the fifteenth century. Once

[200] STC 5542.3.
[201] Wilkins (ed.), *Concilia*, III, 722–23.
[202] On the authorized grammar, see STC 15610.5–6.

established, it continued to be the object of outside forces. Its staff were affected by career opportunities elsewhere, and its teaching by the printed books it used. Disease caused scholars to leave the school, enforced the school to move or close, or killed off pupils and masters. All this should remind us that the schools of the Renaissance period were not just stately galleons blown by a fair wind to a new world, as they have so often been portrayed. They were frail vessels too, tossed by social and economic forces, as they are today.

It is harder to estimate the impact of Magdalen and its fellow schools on Tudor England. Even today, when we believe that schools have great potential to affect society, we often disagree about how they do so. There are, however, ways in which Magdalen School seems at least to reflect the cultural developments in the early sixteenth century, and (perhaps) to forward them. First, the school (like England) experienced an increasing influence from the Continent. In the fifteenth century, culture in England was strongly insular in character. There were indeed external influences from the continental Church and from writers and artists. But one is mostly struck by the Englishness of developments: perpendicular architecture, religious literature in English, individual collegiate foundations (like Magdalen), and England's home-grown heresy, Lollardy. In the sixteenth century, the influence from across the Channel, whether it came from Henry's quarrel with the Pope, from Luther, from Calvin, or from the Catholic Reformation, was very strong. The schools played a part in the opening up of England to such influences. The humanist schoolmasters were more closely linked to contemporary writers on the Continent than their predecessors like Leland had been. Anwykyll drew on Valla and Perotti. Grammars and texts by Mantuan, Perotti, and Sulpizio from Italy, and by De Spouter, Erasmus, and Schade from northern Europe, were widely used in English schools later on.

Next, early Tudor schools anticipate one of the great emphases of most sixteenth-century Church leaders: uniformity. Religious uniformity, in particular, was stressed more in the sixteenth century than before. Just to consider England, there was more codifying of religious belief — the Six Articles of 1539 and the Thirty-Nine Articles of 1563; more uniformity of worship in the Books of Common Prayer of 1549–53; and more stringent measures against dissenters, including more executions. No doubt this was, in large part, the result of religious dissension. Protestants and Catholics alike were led, by confidence or disagreement, to lay more stress on everyone believing and worshipping in the same way. Printing too, was an important factor. It both produced diversity and provided the means for imposing uniformity upon it. Without saying that the idea of uniformity was invented in schools or for schools, it is worth pointing out that uniformity was first attempted in the 1520s in the school sector. Wolsey's grammar and the London decree of 1530 anticipated by several years the application of uniformity to belief and by two decades its extension to worship in church.

Finally, schools were involved with an important change in the ambitions of their pupils which took place between about 1480 and 1520. This concerns pupils who intended to follow lay careers when they left school. Since Anglo-Saxon times, schools in England had taught not only boys who became clergy but boys who remained laity: nobility, gentry, merchants, secretarial clerks, and so on. Kings like Henry IV or Edward IV and their lay nobility in the fifteenth century had studied Latin grammar in their childhood. They were not very latinate in their adulthood, however. They knew, presumably, something about the prayer books which they used for mass or for saying the hours of the Virgin; they could decipher a Latin account or charter if they had to. But, for preference, they wrote and read in English or French. The layman with an ability to write in Latin in the fifteenth century, like Sir John Fortescue, is a rarity, and he was a lawyer accustomed to reading the language. Now, the change from the late-medieval to the humanist curriculum in schools coincided with an increase of lay ambition. Noble and gentle boys continued to go to school to be prepared for lay careers, but more of them aimed to become more highly latinate. This change is first visible, as far as I know, in the family of Henry VII. Though one must be careful not to argue too much from scanty evidence, it looks as though Henry was more ambitious for the education of his sons Arthur and Henry in Latin than Edward IV had been for his children. By the time Arthur died in 1502, at the age of sixteen, he is said to have read twenty-four Latin grammarians and authors. Admittedly, the information comes from his schoolmaster, who had a vested interest in the matter! But the list — the Italian Renaissance grammarians Guarino, Perotti, Sulpizio, and Valla, and a variety of classical authors: Caesar, Cicero, Livy, Lucan, Ovid, Pliny, Sallust, and Virgil — is of a scope impossible to match (even as a plan) for any other English prince since the twelfth century.[203]

We know less about the education of Henry VIII. He started under Skelton, who taught him to spell — presumably elementary learning, but probably also some Latin. After that he had two professional graduate Latin masters, John

[203] On this subject, see Nicholas Orme, *From Childhood to Chivalry: the Education of the English Kings and Aristocracy, 1066–1530* (London, 1984), esp. pp. 149–56.

Holt and William Hoone, both of whom had taught in leading schools (Hoone had followed Holt at Chichester School).[204] When Henry grew up, he posed as a Latinist equal in learning to the clergy. He was credited with writing a famous treatise defending the sacraments against Luther. He authorized the English Bible of 1539, and he discoursed on theology in Parliament in 1540 during the passage of the Act of Six Articles. Kings of England had intervened in Church affairs ever since Ethelbert of Kent in 597. Their interventions, most of which were about matters of appointments, taxation, law, or politics, were usually successful. Henry VIII, Edward VI, and James I, however, claimed an authority over the Church that was intellectual as well as administrative, and they could hardly have done so without good Latin schooling. Nor could their parliaments. A better command of Latin gave the aristocracy parity with the clergy. It enabled the monarch to assert himself, and be widely accepted, as leader of the Church, and for monarch and parliament to be arbiters of theology and worship as well as politics and government.

And Magdalen's part in all this? It was at least threefold. Magdalen educated Wolsey who started to make grammar uniform. It educated William Lily, on whose work the first uniform grammar was based. And through John Holt, it educated Henry VIII who authorized that grammar. Magdalen College and School are an example of the paradox, so common in history, by which a foundation which was meant to promote one kind of culture helped to turn that culture into something different.

[204] Ibid., pp. 23–24; D.R. Carlson, 'Royal Tutors in the Reign of Henry VII', *Sixteenth Century Journal*, 22 (1991), 264–73.

APPENDIX 1

A Revised List of Masters and Ushers of Magdalen School, 1480–1550

This list is based chiefly on Magdalen College Archives (hereafter MCA), Libri Computi, LCE/1–4. These records, the annual accounts of the college, are sometimes undated or equivocally dated, which has misled some earlier historians, notably Bloxam, who was the first to use them and whose suggested dates have been widely copied. The present list is based on a fresh appraisal of all the accounts, which can now be more accurately dated; it contains several names and dates which differ from those given by Bloxam, Emden, and Stanier. The accounts sometimes begin at Michaelmas (29 September) and sometimes at St Martin's Day (11 November). I have assumed, however, that masters and ushers who are listed on 11 November were in office by the previous 29 September when the school and university term began, so all autumn dates below are given as Michaelmas. Surnames are spelt in a standardized form, normally that used by Emden. Christian names are given without brackets when they occur in the Libri Computi and within brackets when they are supplied from other sources, with a question mark when the identity is conjectural.

1. Masters

John Anwykyll. Occurs Michaelmas 1483 (CP 8/49 fol. 16^{r}); vacated through death Christmas 1487 (LCE/1, fols 140^{v}, 156^{r}, 159^{r}).

Two un-named men acted as temporary masters from Christmas 1487 to Easter 1488 (LCE/1, fol. 159^{r}).

[**John**] **Stanbridge**. Appointed Easter 1488 (LCE/1, fols 140^{v}, 159^{r}, 161^{v}), occurs Christmas 1491 (MCA, LCE/2, fol. 15), probably vacated by Michaelmas 1493 (see above, pp. 17–18) and certainly by Michaelmas 1494 (LCE/2, fols 23^{v}–24^{r}). Previously usher. See *BRUO* III, 1754–55.

[**Andrew**] **Scarbot**. Occurs Michaelmas 1494 (LCE/2, fols 23^{v}–24^{r}), vacated (probably through death) Easter 1499 (LCE/2, fol. 91^{v}). See *BRUO* III, 1651.

[**Thomas**] **Wolsey**. Appointed, probably as temporary master, Easter 1499, vacated Michaelmas 1499 (LCE/2, fol. 91^{v}).

[**Richard**] **Jackson**. Probably appointed Michaelmas 1499 (LCE/2, fol. 91^{v}), occurs Michaelmas 1501 (ibid., fol. 105^{r}), vacated by Michaelmas 1502 (ibid., fol. 123^{r}). See *BRUO* II, 1010.

[**Thomas**] **Brinknell**. Occurs Michaelmas 1502 (LCE/2, fol. 123^{r}), vacated about Christmas 1507 (LCE/2, fol. 213^{v}). See *BRUO* I, 268.

[**Nicholas**] **Burway**. Appointed about Christmas 1507 or early 1508 (LCE/2, fols 213^{v}–14^{v}), vacated Michaelmas 1508 (ibid.). See *BRUO* I, 322.

[**Robert**] **Moore**. Appointed Michaelmas 1508 (LCE/2, fol. 229^{r}), vacated Michaelmas 1510 (LCE/3, fol. 4^{r}), or Michaelmas 1512 if he is the 'M. Mores' who occurs between 1510 and 1512 (ibid., fol. 20^{r}, 22^{v}). Previously usher. See *BRUO* IV, 399.

Maurice Lewyt. Appointed Michaelmas 1510 if he is 'M. Mores' (LCE/3, fols 20^{r}, 22^{v}), or else Michaelmas 1512 (ibid., fols 31^{v}, 32^{r}), vacated between Michaelmas 1513 and Michaelmas 1514 (ibid., fol. 44). See *BRUO* IV, 367.

[John?] Haley. Appointed between Michaelmas 1513 and Michaelmas 1514 (LCE/3, fol. 44), vacated Michaelmas 1517 (ibid., fols 104^{v}–05^{r}). Previously usher. See *BRUO* IV, 277.

[Thomas] Stanbridge. Appointed Michaelmas 1517 (LCE/3, fol. 121), occurs Michaelmas 1521 (ibid., fols 165^{v}-66^{r}), vacated by Michaelmas 1524 (ibid., fols 184^{v}–85^{r}), probably through death between Michaelmas 1523 and Michaelmas 1524 (*BRUO* IV, 533).

Vesope/Wesope. Occurs Michaelmas 1524 (LCE/3, fols 184^{v}–85^{r}), vacated between Michaelmas 1526 and Michaelmas 1527 (ibid., fol. 220^{r}). Usually identified with Thomas Bishop, as by Emden, *BRUO* IV, 94, since Bishop's name is spelt Vysshop in other records. Perhaps his surname was something like Westhope, misunderstood as Bishop.

[Thomas] Robertson. Appointed between Michaelmas 1526 and Michaelmas 1527 (LCE/3, fol. 220^{r}), occurs up to about Midsummer or Michaelmas 1531 (LCE/4, fols 18^{v}, 19^{v}), vacated between then and Christmas 1531 (see next entry). See *BRUO* IV, 487.

[Richard] Sherrey. Appointed between about Michaelmas 1531 and January 1532 (see previous entry and *BRUO* IV, 514), occurs Michaelmas 1532 (LCE/4, fols 41^{r}, 42^{r}), vacated Michaelmas 1540 (ibid., fols 145^{v}, 146^{v}). See *BRUO* IV, 514.

Godall. Appointed Michaelmas 1540 (LCE/4, fols 156r, 157r), vacated Michaelmas 1541 (ibid.). Possibly John Godall: see below, section 3, Thornton College.

[John] Harley. Appointed Michaelmas 1541 (LCE/4, fols 168^{r}, 169^{v}), vacated Michaelmas 1547 (LCE/5, fols 40^{r}, 41^{v}). See *BRUO* IV, 266–67.

[John] Slade. Appointed Michaelmas 1547 (LCE/5, fols 53^{r}, 54^{v}), vacated during the year Michaelmas 1548 to Michaelmas 1549 (ibid., fol. 70^{r}). Previously usher.

[Thomas] Cooper. Appointed during the year Michaelmas 1548 to Michaelmas 1549 (LCE/5, fol. 70^{r}), occurs Michaelmas 1555 (ibid., fols 173^{r}, 175^{r}), vacated by Michaelmas 1557 (ibid., fols 200^{r}, 202b). See *BRUO* IV, 135–36.

2. *Ushers*

[John] Stanbridge. Probably appointed Easter 1486, when he left New College (New College Archives, 9746 (Registrum Protocollorum 1455–95), p. 483), occurs Michaelmas 1487 (LCE/1, fol. 140^{v}), promoted to master Easter 1488 (LCE/1, fols 140^{v}, 159^{r}, 161^{v}). See *BRUO* III, 1754–55.

[William?] Ashe. Appointed Easter 1488 (LCE/1, fols 140^{v}, 164^{r}), still in Midsummer term 1489 (LCE/1, fol. 172^{v}). See *BRUO* I, 55.

[John] Holt. Occurs Michaelmas 1494 (MCA, LCE/2, fol. 24^{r}), vacated Easter 1495 (LCE/2, fol. 38^{r}). See *BRUO* II, 953–54.

Howell. Appointed Easter 1495, vacated end of Easter term 1495 (LCE/2, fol. 38^{r}). Bloxam's Christian-name suggestion, John, is unlikely (Bloxam, III, 19).

Two unnamed men acted during Midsummer term 1495 (LCE/2, fol. 38^{r}).

[John] Stokesley. Acted for one month in Michaelmas term 1496 (LCE/2, fol. 77^{r}). See *BRUO* III, 1785–86.

Turne (not Turner). Occurs apparently in Michaelmas term 1496 (LCE/2, fol. 76^{v}).

William Andrew. Occurs apparently in Christmas term 1496–97, Easter term 1497, and part of Midsummer term 1497 (LCE/2, fols 67^{v}, 76^{v}).

Claydon. Occurs apparently in the latter part of Midsummer term 1497 (LCE/2, fol. 76^{v}).

Edward Martyn. Occurs Michaelmas 1498, vacated Midsummer 1499 (LCE/2, fol. 91^{v}).

John Goldyve. Appointed Midsummer 1499 (LCE/2, fol. 91^{v}), vacated by Michaelmas 1500 (LCE/2, fol. 105^{r}).

[**Laurence**] **Hampton**. Occurs from Michaelmas 1500 to Michaelmas 1501 (LCE/2, fol. 105^{r}), vacated by Michaelmas 1502 (ibid., fol. 123). A Laurence Hampton occurs in British Library, Arundel MS 249, fol. 81^{r} — a MS associated with Magdalen College.

[**William**] **Borowe**. Occurs Michaelmas 1502 (LCE/2, fol. 123), vacated Midsummer 1504 (LCE/2, fols 137^{v}–38^{r}). See *BRUO* I, 223.

[**Robert**] **Moore**. Appointed Midsummer 1504 (LCE/2, fols 137^{v}–38^{r}), vacated Christmas 1504–05 (ibid., fols 169^{v}, 170^{r}). Later master. See *BRUO* IV, 399.

John Goldyve. Reappointed about Christmas 1504–05 (LCE/2, fols 169^{v}, 170^{r}), vacated Michaelmas 1505 (ibid.).

[**John?**] **Haley**. Appointed Michaelmas 1505 (LCE/2, fols 182^{v}, 183^{v}), vacated Michaelmas 1506 (ibid.). Later master. See *BRUO* IV, 277.

Felde. Appointed Michaelmas 1506 (LCE/2, fols 197^{r}, 198^{v}), vacated between Michaelmas 1508 and Michaelmas 1509 (ibid., fol. 230^{r}).

[**Richard?**] **Fuller**. Appointed between Michaelmas 1508 and Michaelmas 1509 (LCE/2, fol. 230^{r}), vacated between Michaelmas 1509 and Michaelmas 1510 (LCE/3, fol. 4^{r}). See *BRUO* IV, 222.

[**David**] **Morgan**. Appointed between Michaelmas 1509 and Michaelmas 1510 (LC/3, fol. 4^{r}), vacated Michaelmas 1515 (ibid., fol. 71). See also the next entry, and *BRUO* IV, 401.

[**Maurice**] **Birchynshaw**. Acted as usher from Michaelmas 1512 to Michaelmas 1514, apparently in tandem with, or as a replacement for, Morgan (LCE/3, fols 32^{r}, 44). See *BRUO* I, 190.

[**John**] **Stokys**. Appointed Michaelmas 1515 (LCE/3, fol. 87), vacated between Michaelmas 1516 and Michaelmas 1517 (ibid., fols 104^{v}, 105^{r}). See *BRUO* IV, 542.

[**William**] **Bedyll**. Appointed and vacated between Michaelmas 1516 and Michaelmas 1517 (LCE/3, fols 104^{v}, 105^{r}). See *BRUO* IV, 36.

[**William?**] **Slu** (not Send, as in Bloxam). Appointed and vacated between Michaelmas 1517 and Michaelmas 1518 (LCE/3, fol. 122^{r}). For William Slow (Sloo), see *BRUO* IV, 519.

[**Philip**] **Fryer**. Appointed between Michaelmas 1517 and Michaelmas 1518 (LCE/3, fol. 122^{r}), still at Michaelmas 1521 (ibid., fols 165^{v}, 166^{r}), probably vacated then in view of his later career at Exeter (Orme, *Education in the West of England*, 56–57; *BRUO* IV, 221).

John Hynde. Occurs Michaelmas 1524 (LCE/3, fols 184^{v}, 185^{r}), vacated between Michaelmas 1525 and Michaelmas 1526 (ibid., fols 203^{r}, 204^{r}). See *BRUO* IV, 311.

[**William**] **Sareson**. Appointed between Michaelmas 1525 and Michaelmas 1526 (LCE/3, fols 203^{r}, 204^{r}), occurs Michaelmas 1527 (ibid., fol. 220^{r}), vacated by Michaelmas 1528 (ibid., fol. 243). See *BRUO* IV, 504.

Pearce. Occurs Michaelmas 1528 (LCE/3, fol. 243), vacated between Michaelmas 1532 and Michaelmas 1533 (LCE/4, fols 41^{r}, 42^{r}).

Armyll. Appointed between Michaelmas 1532 and Michaelmas 1533 (LCE/4, fols 41^{r}, 42^{r}), apparently vacated between Michaelmas 1534 and Michaelmas 1535 (ibid., fols 71^{v}, 72^{r}).

[**Ralph**] **Smallpage**. Apparently appointed between Michaelmas 1534 and Michaelmas 1535 (LCE/4, fols 71^{v}, 72^{r}), occurs Michaelmas 1535 (ibid., fol. 72^{r}), vacated by Michaelmas 1536 (ibid., fols 89^{r}, 94^{r}). See *BRUO* IV, 520–21.

[**John**] **Heron/Herne**. Occurs Michaelmas 1536 (LCE/4, fols 89^{r}, 94^{r}), apparently vacated about Easter 1539 (ibid., fol. 129^{r}). See *BRUO* IV, 282.

[**Richard**] **Dighton**. Appointed about Easter 1539, vacated Michaelmas 1539 (LCE/4, fols 129^{r}, 130^{v}). See *BRUO* IV, 181–82.

[**William**] **Hewis**. Appointed Michaelmas 1539 (LCE/4, fols 145^{v}, 146^{v}), vacated between about Midsummer and Michaelmas 1545 (LCE/5, fols 16^{r}, 17^{r}). See *BRUO* IV, 287.

[**John**] **Slade**. Appointed Michaelmas 1545 (LCE/5, fols 27^{r}, 28^{r}), promoted as master Michaelmas 1547 (LCE/5, fols 40^{r}, 41^{v}). See Boase, *Register*, 209.

[**John**] **Bolderne**. Appointed Michaelmas 1547 (LCE/5, fols 53^{r}, 54^{v}), vacated Michaelmas 1549 (ibid., fols 69^{r}, 70^{r}). See Boase, *Register*, 206.

[**Robert**] **Lillye**. Appointed Michaelmas 1549 (LCE/5, fol. 85), occurs Michaelmas 1553 (ibid., fols 144^{v}, 146^{v}), vacated by Michaelmas 1554 (ibid., fols 173^{r}, 175^{r}). See Boase, *Register*, 213.

APPENDIX 2

Masters of Magdalen College School, Wainfleet, 1466–1555

There is a useful recent history of this school by Brenda Parry-Jones and Derrick Wales, *Five Hundred Years of Magdalen College School Wainfleet 1484–1984* (Wainfleet, 1984). The following references, unless otherwise indicated, come from the Magdalen College Archives.

John Marshall. Paid from November to November [1464–65?] in an account of 1 January 1466 to 1 May 1467 (EP/165/6), still at Michaelmas 1469 (EP/165/3).

Thomas Whetley. Occurs Michaelmas 1479 (EP/165/20), still at Michaelmas 1481 (EP/165/11; EP/165/20).

Thomas Bowcher. Chaplain; occurs from Michaelmas 1481 to Michaelmas 1482 (EP/165/11; EP/165/14).

William Hode. Occurs from Michaelmas 1483 (EP/138/13) to 6 October 1491 (EP/183/15); perhaps until Michaelmas 1495. Hode was also rector of Wainfleet All Saints, 1458–95.

William Dobyll. Occurs from Michaelmas 1493 (EP/184/12) to Michaelmas 1495 (EP/184/5).

Thomas Brinknell. Occurs from (perhaps appointed) Michaelmas 1495 (EP/184/20) to Michaelmas 1500 (EP/185/2). See *BRUO* I, 268.

[Richard?] Ranson. Occurs 1526 (*A Subsidy Collected in the Diocese of Lincoln in 1526*, ed. H.E. Salter, Oxford Historical Society, LXIII (1909), 3). The name is there transcribed as 'Rauson', but Richard Ranson occurs as rector of Wainfleet All Saints by 1530, and bequeathed six books to Wainfleet School in his will of 1549 (London, Public Record Office, Prob 11/32, fols 333^{v}–34^{v} (43 Populwell)).

[William] Shallock. Occurs 1535 (*Valor Ecclesiasticus tempore Henrici VIII*, ed. J. Caley, 6 vols (London: Record Commission, 1810–24), ii. 281). See *BRUO* IV, 512.

William Richardson. Appointed 1555 (Macray, *Register*, II, 31).

APPENDIX 3

Links between Magdalen College and Schools Elsewhere in England, 1480–1540

1. Places

Banbury, Oxon. John Stanbridge, Thomas Brinknell, Thomas Stanbridge, Nicholas Cartwright, all studied or taught at both Magdalen and Banbury schools (*BRUO* I, 268; III. 1754–55; IV, 105–06, 533.

Beaulieu Abbey, Hants. A letter from J.H. [John Holt?] to H.B. (or H.S.), *c.*1500, in a letter collection associated with Magdalen College, contains the offer of a teaching post at the abbey (British Library, Arundel MS 249, fol. 86r).

Brackley, Northants. Thomas Godwin, fellow of Magdalen 1545–49, was headmaster of Brackley School 1549–52 (*BRUO* IV, 237), and was succeeded by Robert Bede, fellow of Magdalen 1541–52, in 1552–58 (ibid., 36).

Bruton, Somerset. The foundation statutes of 1520 ordered grammar to be taught according to the usage of Magdalen College Oxford or St Paul's School London (Orme, *Education in the West of England*, p. 121).

Chichester, Sussex. John Holt was master of this school, 1501–02 (*BRUO* II, 953–54), and John Goldyve in 1521 (ibid., II, 788).

Chipping Campden, Glos. James Dodman, demy of Magdalen 1532–35, was master of this school in 1542 (*BRUO* IV, 170).

Eton, Berks. John Goldyve was master of this school, 1507–10 (*BRUO* II, 788).

Evesham, Worcs. Robert Lyster, fellow of Magdalen 1520–24, was schoolmaster of Evesham in 1524 (*BRUO* IV, 370).

Exeter, Devon. William Andrew, usher of Magdalen College School, was probably master of Exeter High School in 1505–06, as was Philip Fryer, usher of Magdalen College School, in 1521 (Orme, *Education in the West of England*, pp. 56–57).

Ipswich, Suffolk. The grammar school was briefly refounded on a larger scale by Thomas Wolsey between 1528 and 1530 (I.E. Gray and W.E. Potter, *Ipswich School, 1450–1950* (Ipswich, 1950), pp. 1–30).

Lichfield, Staffs. John Stanbridge may have been a master at this school in the 1490s, in view of his links with William Smith, bishop of Lichfield, and Robert Whittington who came from the city.

London, Lambeth Palace. John Holt taught in the household school of John Morton, archbishop of Canterbury, from Easter 1496 until not later than about 1500 (Nicholas Orme, 'John Holt', pp. 287–89).

London, St Paul's School. William Lily was the first high master of this school, 1509/1512–22 (Sir Michael McDonnell, *The Registers of St Paul's School 1509–1748* (London, 1977), pp. 1–2; *BRUO* II, 1147), and Maurice Birchynshaw was sur-master (second master) in 1515–17 (*BRUO* I, 90; McDonnell, p. 3).

Oxford, Cardinal College. Richard Sherrey, demy of Magdalen 1522, was grammar master of the choristers of Cardinal College *c.*1530 (*BRUO* IV, 514).

Rochester, Kent. John Heron, usher of Magdalen College School 1537–39, was headmaster of King's School Rochester in 1552 (*BRUO* IV, 282).

Thornton Curtis, Lincs. Godall (Christian name unknown), who was master of Magdalen College School from 1541 to 1542, may well be identical with John Goodall, master of Thornton College grammar school in 1548 (Leach, *English Schools at the Reformation*, pt ii, p. 135).

Trowbridge, Wilts. Robert Wheteacre, chaplain of Magdalen 1534, probationary fellow 1542, was master of the grammar school from about 1542, and still in 1548 (*BRUO* IV, 620; Orme, *Education in the West of England*, pp. 171–72).

Wainfleet, Lincs. The school was closely connected with Magdalen College, which is recorded appointing schoolmasters in 1494–95 and 1555 (Macray, I, 26; II, 31). William Dobyll, master of the school in 1493–95, may be identical with the Dobyll who occurs as a chorister and demy of Magdalen from 1485 to 1493–94 (Parry-Jones and Wales, *Magdalen College School Wainfleet*, 7; *BRUO* I, 580). His successor, Thomas Brinknell, master in 1495–1500, was an alumnus of Lincoln College not Magdalen, though he subsequently had a close connection with the college (Parry-Jones and Wales, *Magdalen College School Wainfleet*, p. 7; *BRUO* I, 268).

Winchcombe Abbey, Glos. John Stanbridge may have taught here *c.* 1493 (above, p. 18).

Unknown. John Morton, chorister of Magdalen 1506, took the schoolmasters' degree of bachelor of grammar 1525, perhaps teaching in Kent or London (*BRUO* IV, 402–03).

2. *Noble Households*

Henry, Prince of Wales (Henry VIII). John Holt was his grammar master, *c.*1502–04 (Orme, 'John Holt', pp. 289–90).

John Dudley, Earl of Warwick. John Harley, ex-fellow of Magdalen and master of the school, was tutor to his children *c.*1548 (*BRUO* IV, 266–67).

Cardinal John Morton. See above, London, Lambeth Palace

Sir John Walsh, of Little Sodbury, Glos. William Tyndale, educated at Magdalen Hall *c.*1512–15, was tutor to his children *c.*1522 (*BRUO* IV, 567–68).

Thomas Winter (son of Cardinal Wolsey). Maurice Birchynshaw was his tutor in the early 1520s (*BRUO* IV, 190).

APPENDIX 4

Letters concerning Scholars at Magdalen College, c.1496–c.1525

In this edition, sentence and word divisions, capital letters and punctuation usually follow modern practice. Abbreviations are expanded in italics, and editorial additions are placed in square brackets.

1. 4 January, probably 1496. Richard Croft, esquire, to Richard Mayew, president of Magdalen College (MCA, MS 367, no. 24). A chorister named Perkins occurs at Magdalen in 1496; no further career is known (Bloxam, *Register*, I, 6). Croft's will, dated 1501, is in *Some Oxfordshire Wills*, ed. J.R.H. Weaver and A. Beardwood, Oxfordshire Record Society, 39 (1958), 72–73.

M*aster* presedentte, aftyr all dewe reu*eren*ce hadde, I am ryȝt glade to here of yo*ur* good p*ro*sperite and rekouery of yo*ur* late grete desese, thanckede be God, of your good comffort, and ou*er* this, s*ir*, hitt *is* so thatte I have a godson wiche is a ten*a*untt*es* son of myn of Chepyng Norton, on' Richard P*er*kyns, wiche I thynck thatt ye have knowlage of, and he is wele enturde in lernyng of his tyme and he is well dissposede to lerne, and pety hitte wyrre butte thatte he hadde good helpe thereto, and therfore I hertely p*r*aye you to be his good m*aster* at this my pore instance and to ecepte hym into yo*ur* place w*ith* siche resonable eccebysion ase is the custewme of yo*ur* plase w*ith* y*our* lovyng favo*ur*, and he shalbe yo*ur* bedman and I at yo*ur* co*m*ma*n*dme*n*t af[t]yr my litylle power all dayse of my lyffe w*ith* God*es* myȝte, whome p*re*serue you and encrese yo*ur* goode heele of body ase I wolde have myselfe. W*ith* the honde of yo*ur* lovyng frende and s*er*uau*n*te, the iiijthe daye of Jenawarie,

Richard Croft] esquire

[Endorsed:] To M' P*re*sedentte of Maudelen Colage in Oxon be this delyuerd.

2. 21 July, *c.*1498. John Etton to President Mayew (MCA, MS 367, no. 16). John Etton occurs as a Magdalen College agent at Grantham in 1494–95 (Macray, *Register*, I, 26). Mayew is first recorded as king's almoner in 1497 (*BRUO* II, 1248). Magdalen College gained full possession of the manor of Candlesby after the death of Maud Lady Willoughby on 30 August 1497.

My most singuler and especiall gudde mayster, j recomaunde me vnto yowre gudde mast*er*schipe, and s*ir*, y pray yowe to be gudde and singuler mayster to my son, the weche y sende to yowre maysterschipe and to be at yowre reulle and gydyng and my cost and scharge, and thatt he may hafe a scharpe creansur to se in especiall to his lernyng and also to his gudde rewlle, for y wolde for no cause bot that he warre conversant w*ith* vertously company and es my speciall truste in yowre mayst*er*schipe, and s*ir*, seche comens as yowre mayst*er*schipe thynkys es metly for hym lat hym be att and y send to deliu*er* to hym thatt ye will aponnte to be his creansur xl s. to pay wekely for his comens and for necessarres that es neddefull for hym, and s*ir*, y schall rewarde hym thatt shall be his creansur be yowre discression thatt he schall hafe cause to do for hym as moche as he schall hafe for eny that he es creansur to for my degre. And s*ir*, y send x li. in mony, trustyng ye will be and all my mayster of yowre college better mayster to hym and yf y [hafe, *deleted*] can do eny better s*er*uise to yowre collegge than y hafe her afor, y schall be redy to my powre. And s*ir*, y truste ye will send yowre audite nowe at michelmas into thys contre, seyng nowe at Muchelmes ye schall enter into the man*er* of Candelesby and take the p*ro*ffitt*es*, seke vppe yowre yndenture thatt Thom*as* Sneth may se it thys wynter, and also to brynge worde who ye will send at Michelmes to be at Saltfletby in vigilia S*anct*i Fid*ei* and so to yowre curtes of Candelesby and Frampton or elles to kepe this courte afor Saltfletby. Wreten the xxj dey of July,

Be yowre s*er*u*a*und
John Etton

[Endorsed:] To the right worschipfull and my gudde Mayster Mayewe, kynges aumear and p*re*sedent of Mawdeleyn College in Oxinford, be thys diliu*er*ed.

3. Between *c*.1504 and 1509. Draft of a letter, perhaps from Robert Yall to John Molesworth, fellow of Magdalen College (Bodleian Library, MS Rawlinson D.913, fol. 105[v]).

Robert Yall

Master Mullysworth, I wold pray *and* beseytt yow that yow wold be my good master, for syche gere as y lerne that yow wold sew ytt to me by feer mense and ponys me resnab[l]y. Now yow ponyse me hou*er* much, master, *and* plese yow y cannott byd *th*is ponysment. Her at fryst tyme yow dyd nott ponyse me nott havff so much; then y dyd lerne more by yowr feyer mense then I doo now.

4. 12 August, perhaps early sixteenth century. Thomas Keys to the President of Magdalen College (MCA, MS 367, no. 26). A Richard Kay or Key graduated as BA in 1523, MA in 1532 (*BRUO* IV, 324).

+ Jhus

Aftu*r* my most lowly maner I reco*m*mende me vnto yo*ur* mast*er*ship. Please it you to vnd*er*stonde I haue ress' j lettur from yo*ur* scoler Richard Keys, whiche lettur is closyd herin, besekyng yo*ur* mast*er*ship that you will send for Rychard Keys and soo to vnd*er*stond wherfor is mastu*r* will put hym from hym as y vnderstond he as put is felow att Ladye [Day] from hym, wherfor, s*ir*, that it will please you to know the serteyn of the cawse, and that he maye be horderd by yo*ur* mast*er*ship as you shall seme most best. Sir, he is but yonge of age and therfor I beseke you he may haue yo*ur* faver, for I ham sewer he woll do muche aftu*r* yo*ur* mynde shewede to hym and as to his batyll maye be synyd by you and I shall se you co*n*tent and as to all hothu*r* chargys that it woll please you that yo*ur* servant Jorge maye sende me worde, I shalt heu*er* be glad to see it done, and of yo*ur* goode answer of this lettu*r* I beseke you, and to be goode mastu*r* to yo*ur* scoler Richard Keys, for he is my cowmford next to God and my lord, and I shall praye to God for my lord *and* yo*ur* maist*er*ship longe to lyve. At Ypuwiche the xii-it d[ay] August. Yo*ur* owne to his power, Thom*as* Keys.

[Endorsed:] To the Ryght Worshipfull Maystu*r* Presydent i*n* Mawdlen Coledge this be d'd.

5. 8 June, probably 1513. From John Burges to John Claymond, president of Magdalen College (MCA, MS 367, no. 42). Simon Beneson, mentioned as wishing to graduate as BA in this letter, did so in the spring of 1514 (*BRUO* IV, 42).

Rygth honoraboll gud maiestr', all dew co*m*mendation p*re*mysid, so it is *th*at I haue rescevid a lett*er* ffro*m* Josepth Beneson wherein he desierd me to speke to yo*ur* maiestreschippe and instantly to desier yow to be so gud m[aiestre] to his sone Symon to lice*n*s hy*m* to co*m*mens *and* to optayne yo*ur* maiestres mynd*es* to the same, ffor he thynkys it g*re*tely to his rebuke *th*at sutch as wer' Symons fellos i*n* Boston hath tor*n*yd home maiesters of art, as Couys son *and* oth*er*, he beyng nat batchulor. He seth he putt*es* hys trust to yow (tho it be vndes*er*uyd) abowe all men of hon*ur* beyng of his acqwayenta*n*s. Wherffor he p*r*ays yow i*n*stantly *tha*t he may p*r*ocede *thi*s mydsom*er*. He wolld gladly haue hy*m* at Boston ffor he se hy*m* nat sens he cam to Oxfford, and his disease is sutch *tha*t he canat ryde to co*m* heth*er*, and he wolld not ffor a c li. he *shu*ld co*m*e home w*ith*owt degree off *th*e schole. And iff his g*r*ace may nat be optayned, he wolld *tha*t he *shu*ld p*r*ocede neu*er* the les. How be it, *tha*t *shu*ld be chargeabyll to hy*m*, as yow know, he seith. Therffor, iff it wolld please yow now havyng *th*e offic*er*s at home to optayne his g*r*ace, yow *shu*ld do hy*m* g*re*t pleser, *and* bynd *them* booth to be yo*ur* beedemen as knowe*s* God, who*m* to kepe yow is my prayer. Fro*m* Brakley, viio die Junii, yo*ur* scholar John Burges.

[Endorsed:] To hys rygth honoraboll gud maiestre, Maiestre P*re*sident.

6. 12 June, between 1521 and 1525. John Constable, priest, to John Higden, president of Magdalen College (MCA, Arch. MS 367, no. 47). The date is defined by the fact that Antony Sutton is called 'master' — he graduated MA in 1521 (*BRUO* IV, 548) — and that Higden ceased to be president in November 1525.

Right honorable brother, I co*m*maund me hartely vnto you, and I am enf*ur*myd that maist*er* Antony Sutton, creanser vnto William Shawe, taketh suche displeaso*ur* with him that he feareth for the same to be putt owte of his rometh that he hath in yo*ur* college at this next mydsom*er*. I suppose it is for some myssedemeano*ur* that he hath done, contrary to your statut*es*, or els for mysse-orderynge him selff vnto his good maist*er* *and* crea*n*ser. And if it so be, I beseche you that his farther, this bearer, my s*er*vaunt, may be pleanly info*ur*myd theroff that he may charge him streyghtly to reforme himselff. How so eu*er* it be, I wold besech you hartely the rather at this myn instau*n*ce to be so good maist*er* vnto him that he vppon his good abearynge myght co*n*tynew in your college one other yere like as he hath done. And if he frome hensfourth doe not exercice himselff in learnyng and v*er*tue, I shall neu*er* entreate more for him thus. I thanke you hartely for the goodnes that ye hetherto haue showyd vnto him, wiche I know well was only for my sake. Thus hartely faire ye well. Frome Lincoln, the twelfth daye of June.

by yo*ur* feythfull brodre
John Constable preest

[Endorsed:] To my right honorable brother Maist*er* docto*ur* Hygden, p*re*sident of Mawdelen Colegg.

BIBLIOGRAPHY

Manuscript Sources

Bury St Edmunds, Suffolk Record Office
  IC 500/2/2 (Hawlee, 189) (Will of Andrew Scarbot, senior)
London, British Library
  Arundel MS 249
  Royal MS 12.B.xx
London, Public Record Office
  Prob 11 (Registered copy wills)
Oxford, Bodleian Library
  MS Rawlinson D.913
Oxford, Magdalen College Archives
  Deeds, Candlesby, 16, 20
  EL/1 (Admission Registers)
  EP/165/3, /6, /11, /14, /20 (Estate Accounts)
  EP/183/15; EP/184/20; EP/185/2 (Estate Accounts)
  F.IX (i) (Edward Chapman, Views of Old Oxford, vol. I)
  LCE/1–5 (Libri Computi)
  MS 367 (Letters volume, now being rebound in fascicules)
  MS 881 (v) (J.R. Bloxam's annotated copy of his *Register*, vol. III)
Oxford, Magdalen College Old Library
  Arch. B.III.1.13 (John Stanbridge's copy of Cicero, *Epistolae Familiares* (Venice, 1485))
  Arch. B.III.4.4–5 (John Stanbridge's copy of Plutarch, *Vitae Illustrium Virorum* (2 vols, Venice, 1478))
Oxford, New College Archives
  NCA 5529 (Liber Senescalli Aulae, 1478–99)
  NCA 9746 (Registrum Protocollorum, 1455–95)
Oxford, University Archives
  Chancery Court Depositions, Hyp/B/2
  Registers of Congregation, G, H

Printed Sources

ALEXANDRE-BIDON, DANIÈLE, 'La Lettre volée: apprendre à lire à l'enfant au moyen âge', *Annales*, 44 (1989), 953–92

ANWYKYLL, JOHN, *Compendium totius grammatice* (Oxford, 1483 and other editions)

BALE, JOHN, *Illustrium Maioris Britanniae Scriptorum* (Wesel, 1548); 2nd edn (Basle, 1557)

BLOXAM, J.R., *A Register of the Presidents, Fellows, Demies . . . and Other Members of St Mary Magdalen College in the University of Oxford*, 8 vols (Oxford, 1853–85)

BOASE, C.W. (ed.), *Register of the University of Oxford*, vol. I *(1449–63; 1505–71)*, Oxford Historical Society, i (1885)

BREEZE, A., and J. GLOMSKI, 'An Early Treatise upon Education: Leonard Cox's *De Erudienda Iuventute* (1526)', *Humanistica Lovaniensia*, 40 (1991), 112–67

BRODIE, A.H., 'Anwykyll's *Vulgaria*': a Pre-Erasmian Textbook', *Neuphilologische Mitteilunge*, 75 (1974), 416–27

BUCKLER, J.C., *Observations on the Original Architecture of Saint Mary Magdalen College, Oxford* (London, 1823)

CARLSON, D.R., 'Royal Tutors in the Reign of Henry VII', *Sixteenth Century Journal*, 22 (1991), 264–73

CATTO, J.I., and RALPH EVANS (eds), *The History of the University of Oxford*, II: *Late Medieval Oxford* (Oxford, 1992)

CAVENDISH, GEORGE, *The Life and Death of Cardinal Wolsey*, ed. by R.S. Sylvester, Early English Text Society, o.s. 243 (1959)

CHANDLER, RICHARD, *The Life of William Waynflete* (London, 1811)

CHITTY, H.F., 'The Second Masters of Winchester College', *The Wykehamist*, no. 551 (April 1916), pp. 2–3

COBBAN, A.B., *The Medieval English Universities: Oxford and Cambridge to c.1500* (Aldershot, 1988)

CONWAY, WILLIAM MARTIN, *The Woodcutters of the Netherlands in the Fifteenth Century* (Cambridge, 1884)

DAVIS, VIRGINIA, *William Waynflete: Bishop and Educationalist* (Woodbridge, 1993)

DURHAM, BRIAN, *et al.*, 'The Infirmary and Hall of the Medieval Hospital of St. John the Baptist at Oxford', *Oxoniensia*, 56 (1991), 17–75

EMDEN, A.B., *A Biographical Register of the University of Oxford to A.D.1500*, 3 vols (Oxford, 1957–59)

——, *A Biographical Register of the University of Oxford A.D. 1501 to 1540* (Oxford, 1974)

——, *An Oxford Hall in Medieval Times* (Oxford, 1927)

FRERE, W.H., and W.M. KENNEDY (eds), *Visitation Articles and Injunctions of the Period of the Reformation*, 3 vols, Alcuin Club Collections, 14–16 (1910)

GWOSDEK, HEDWIG (ed.), *Early Printed Editions of the Long Accidence and Short Accidence Grammars* (Heidelberg, 1991)

HODNETT, EDWARD, *English Woodcuts 1480–1535*, 2nd edn (Oxford, 1973)

HUNT, R.W., 'Oxford Grammar Masters of the Later Middle Ages', *Oxford Studies Presented to Daniel Callus*, Oxford Historical Society, n.s. 16 (1964), 163–93

KIRBY, T.F., *Winchester Scholars* (London and Winchester, 1888)

LEACH, A.F., *English Schools at the Reformation, 1546–8* (Westminster, 1896)

——, *Educational Charters and Documents, 598–1909* (Cambridge, 1911)

——, *The Schools of Medieval England*, 2nd edn (London, 1915)

LEATHES, S.M. (ed.), *Grace Book A*, Luard Memorial Series, I (Cambridge, 1897)

LLOYD, A.H., *The Early History of Christ's College Cambridge* (Cambridge, 1934)

LYTE, H.C. MAXWELL, *A History of Eton College (1440–1910)*, 4th edn (London, 1911)

MCCONICA, JAMES (ed.), *The History of the University of Oxford*, III: *The Collegiate University* (Oxford, 1986)

MACRAY, W.D., *A Register of the Members of St. Mary Magdalen College, Oxford*, n.s., 8 vols (London, 1894–1915)

NELSON, WILLIAM (ed.), *A Fifteenth Century School Book* (Oxford, 1956)

ORME, NICHOLAS, *English Schools in the Middle Ages* (London, 1973)

——, *Education in the West of England, 1066–1548* (Exeter, 1976)

——, 'An Early-Tudor Oxford Schoolbook', *Renaissance Quarterly*, 34 (1981), 11–39

——, *From Childhood to Chivalry: the Education of the English Kings and Aristocracy, 1066–1530* (London, 1984)

——, *Education and Society in Medieval and Renaissance England* (London and Ronceverte, 1989)

——, 'An English Grammar School ca. 1450: Latin Exercises from Exeter (Caius College MS 417/447, folios 16v–24v)', *Traditio*, 1 (1995), 261–94

——, 'John Holt (d. 1504), Tudor Schoolmaster and Grammarian', *The Library*, 6th ser. 18 (1996), 283–305

——, and Margaret Webster, *The English Hospital 1070–1570* (New Haven and London, 1995)

Pantin, W.A., 'Abbot Kidderminster and Monastic Studies', *Downside Review*, 47 (1929), 199–211

Parry-Jones, Brenda, and Derrick Wales, *Five Hundred Years of Magdalen College School Wainfleet 1484–1984* (Wainfleet, 1984)

Pollard, A.W., and G.R. Redgrave (comps), *A Short-Title Catalogue of Books Printed in England . . . 1475–1640*, 2nd edn, ed., rev., and enlarged by W.A. Jackson, F.S. Ferguson, and K.F. Pantzer, 3 vols (London, 1967–91)

Salter, H.E. (ed.), *Registrum Annalium Collegii Mertonensis, 1483–1521*, Oxford Historical Society, 86 (1923)

Seaborne, Malcolm, *The English School: Its Architecture and Organization 1370–1870* (London, 1971)

Stanier, R.S., *A History of Magdalen College School, Oxford*, 2nd edn (Oxford, 1958)

Statuta Antiqua Vniversitatis Oxon, ed. by Strickland Gibson (Oxford, 1931)

Statutes of the Colleges of Oxford, II: Magdalen College (Oxford and London, 1853)

Sterry, Sir Wasey, *The Eton College Register, 1441–1698* (Eton, 1943)

Thomson, David, *A Descriptive Catalogue of Middle English Grammatical Texts* (New York and London, 1979)

——, *An Edition of the Middle English Grammatical Texts* (New York and London, 1984)

——, 'The Oxford Grammar Masters Revisited', *Mediaeval Studies*, 45 (1983), 298–310

Valor Ecclesiasticus tempore Henrici VIII auctoritate regis institutus, ed. by J. Caley, 6 vols (London, 1810–24)

The Victoria History of the Counties of England: Oxfordshire, ed. by H.E. Salter and Mary Lobel, III (London, 1954)

Ward, G.R.M. (ed.), *The Statutes of Magdalen College Oxford* (Oxford, 1840)

Weiss, R., *Humanism in England during the Fifteenth Century*, 3rd edn (Oxford, 1967)

White, Beatrice (ed.), *The Vulgaria of John Stanbridge and the Vulgaria of Robert Whittinton*, Early English Text Society, o.s. 187 (London, 1932)

Wilkins, D. (ed.), *Concilia Magnae Britanniae et Hiberniae, 446–1717*, 4 vols (London, 1737)

Wood, Anthony, *The History and Antiquities of the Colleges and Halls in the University of Oxford*, ed. by J. Gutch, 5 vols (Oxford, 1786–90)

——, *Athenae Oxonienses*, ed. by P. Bliss, 4 vols (London, 1813–20)

INDEX

The terms 'demy', 'fellow', 'master', 'president', and 'usher' relate to Magdalen College Oxford and its school.